Sarah Stow

Semi-centennial celebration of Mount Holyoke Seminary

South Hadley, Mass., 1837-1887

Sarah Stow

Semi-centennial celebration of Mount Holyoke Seminary
South Hadley, Mass., 1837-1887

ISBN/EAN: 9783741155918

Manufactured in Europe, USA, Canada, Australia, Japa

Cover: Foto ©Lupo / pixelio.de

Manufactured and distributed by brebook publishing software (www.brebook.com)

Sarah Stow

Semi-centennial celebration of Mount Holyoke Seminary

SEMI-CENTENNIAL

CELEBRATION

OF

MOUNT HOLYOKE SEMINARY,

SOUTH HADLEY, MASS.

1837-1887.

EDITED BY
Mrs. SARAH LOCKE STOW, of '59.

PUBLISHED BY THE SEMINARY.
1888.

MT. HOLYOKE SEMINARY

SEMI-CENTENNIAL.

PREPARATIONS.

PRELIMINARIES for the celebration of the fiftieth anniversary of Mt. Holyoke Seminary in 1887 were referred by the trustees to a committee appointed at their annual meeting in June, 1884, and reappointed a year later.

The president of the board, Rev. Wm. S. Tyler, D. D., was engaged to prepare the historical address, and measures were taken to secure the publication of a history of the seminary during its first half-century.

Two semi-centennial days were observed in 1886. The first was February 10*, when the granting of the seminary charter was commemorated by an exercise in the seminary hall, of which the chief features were the reading of the act of incorporation, a brief account of the obstacles that had to be overcome before it could be secured, with fitting mention of the historical importance of the event; for before 1836 but two institutions, for girls only, had been chartered in the Commonwealth, Ipswich Academy in 1828, and Abbot Academy in 1829; the former had no endowment to secure its continued existence, and the latter was not designed exclusively to furnish the higher education, and for nearly forty years required no examinations for admission; while the charter of Mt. Holyoke Seminary legalized the holding of funds gathered—though with great

---

* The bill granting the charter passed both branches of the Legislature, February 10, 1836, and was signed by the Governor—Edward Everett—on the next day. But in 1886, the 11th came on Sunday.

opposition and ridicule—to found a permanent institution, designed to do for young women what colleges for two hundred years had been doing for young men.

These funds were the voluntary gifts of benevolence and were all spent in building. In the entire lack of endowed departments, running expenses had been met for half a century from board and tuition fees; these were kept at the lowest figure practicable, that the seminary course might be " within reach of the class most likely to be benefited by it and to use it for the good of the world." In view of these facts, when the desire of making a jubilee gift to their *alma mater* was expressed in the annual meeting of the National Association of Holyoke Alumnæ, June, 1885, the proposition to secure endowment for the chair of the Principal met with a warm response, and it was resolved to raise for this purpose before June, 1887, the sum of $20,000, to be called the Mary Lyon Fund. To devise means for its accomplishment a committee was appointed of which Mrs. Helen French Gulliver was chairman. Early in 1886 Mrs. Gulliver sent " to the widely scattered pupils of Mt. Holyoke Seminary " a letter gratefully acknowledging their former gifts to the seminary,—by means of which not only had no slight degree of progress been made, but comfort and convenience had been greatly increased,—and earnestly soliciting their co-operation in the inauguration of a new era in the life of the institution by providing the first endowment fund.

Prompt responses came from numerous donors, who gladly contributed in proportion to their ability. In January, 1887, $7,300 had been received and invested. At that time, the alumnæ were furnished—for use in their appeals to others—with circulars issued by the trustees and a committee of the alumnæ, setting forth the worthy work of the seminary and urging not only the speedy completion of the Mary Lyon fund of $20,000, but the need of an instruction fund of not less than $100,000.

The result is recorded in Mrs. Gulliver's report at the jubilee gathering.

PREPARATIONS.

The other event commemorated in 1886 was the laying of the corner-stone,—at the northwest corner of the main building,—which took place, according to the letters of invitation, "at two o'clock on Monday, October 3, 1836, with appropriate religious exercises and an address by Rev. John Todd." Eye witnesses relate that General Asa Howland of Conway used the mortar and laid the stone, depositing, with other papers in the place prepared, the names of Mary Lyon and the trustees. The fiftieth return of that date fell on the Sabbath, and was observed by an evening service in the seminary hall, conducted by Rev. W. S. Hawks of South Hadley Falls, whose memorial sermon was pointed with lessons drawn from a sketch of the life of Mary Lyon.

In 1886 also hundreds of alumnæ, with gifts to the Mary Lyon fund, contributed reminiscences and testimony for use in preparing the semi-centennial history of the seminary, which was published in time for sale at the jubilee.

Another undertaking of great labor was the preparation, for delivery at the same time, of the tenth "Five Years' Catalogue" of the Memorandum Society, in which Mrs. Pease, the secretary, reported information concerning the two thousand graduates and over one thousand other members of the society. To reach all who were living of the more than three thousand other alumnæ,—the term alumnæ being used in this pamphlet to include all former students whether graduates or not,—the following notice was inserted in the annual catalogue of 1886 :—

TO FORMER STUDENTS.

In view of the approaching Semi-Centennial of Mt. Holyoke Seminary in June, 1887, an effort is being made to obtain the addresses of all who have ever been its students. All who receive this catalogue will aid in this great work by sending at once their own addresses and those of all pupils known to them who are not members of the Memorandum Society, to MRS. C. B. PEASE, Somers, Conn.

In January, 1887, the trustees through their committee issued the following circular letter, which was sent to all alumnæ whose addresses were known, about forty-five hundred in number.

MOUNT HOLYOKE SEMINARY.

1837–1887.

DEAR FRIEND :—

You are cordially invited to attend the Semi-Centennial Celebration of the Seminary, June 22 and 23, 1887.

Tuesday evening will be devoted to exchanging greetings in the seminary hall.

Wednesday morning there will be class meetings, and at 10 o'clock a family gathering in church, for addresses from representatives of the various classes. At 2 P. M., there will be a meeting of the Alumnæ Association, in church.

Thursday A. M. the anniversary exercises will be held, in a tent on the seminary grounds. Historical address by Rev. W. S. Tyler, D. D.

This circular is intended to be sent to every person who has been connected with the seminary. Husbands will be welcomed with their wives.

Hotel accommodations can be obtained at Springfield, Holyoke, and Northampton, and means of transportation to and from the seminary. The people of the vicinity will receive as many as they can entertain, and a large number of cot-beds will probably be provided in rooms near the seminary, for those who will be content with such accommodations. A restaurant tent on the grounds will furnish meals at reasonable rates.

Although June seems yet some distance in the future, it is important that we receive immediate answers stating your intention and the probability of your being present, that we may perfect our plans.

A second circular containing further particulars will be sent a short time previous to the celebration, but to those only who respond to this.

Please send reply to MISS E. BLANCHARD, South Hadley, Mass.

> A. L. WILLISTON,
> G. H. WHITCOMB,
> E. HITCHCOCK,
> MISS E. BLANCHARD,
> MRS. A. L. WILLISTON,
>
> *Committee of Arrangements.*

SOUTH HADLEY, MASS., JAN. 20, 1887.

Members of the Memorandum Society and many others responded readily to the request for aid in obtaining addresses. For months Mrs. Pease and Miss Edwards labored to make the list complete. But lest, after all effort, some should fail to receive a personal message, notices were inserted in the newspapers extending the invitation to all former students.

Plans for the entertainment of guests were early arranged. Before snow left the ground a canvass of the village and surrounding districts for lodging places began. The teachers who engaged in it came back from each half-day's tour with but one report. As at the twenty-fifth anniversary, the hospitable citizens—and there were no others—opened wide their doors. Several families offered to receive forty lodgers each; others agreed to provide respectively for the alumnæ of given years, supplementing home resources by cot-beds if necessary.

The committee of arrangements held frequent meetings and were in constant conference between meetings. The gentlemen of the committee took in charge the provision of cot-beds and blankets; arrangements for tents and a caterer; and negotiations with hotels, stage drivers, and railways. Mr. Williston especially spared neither time nor pains in perfecting plans and securing their execution. Telephonic communication with his office in Northampton was in frequent use.

To all who replied to the first circular a second was sent in May, announcing transportation, lodging, and restaurant rates; terms secured at hotels in Holyoke and Springfield; time tables and reduced railway rates. In the same inclosures were sent cards with blanks to be filled and returned—naming the time of intended arrival. On the return of these cards "stage lists" were arranged and conveyances engaged accordingly for arrivals by each train; lodging places were assigned and reported to both host and guest; and corresponding entry was made in the various books of record. Students caught the enthusiasm and aided in the innumerable details of preparation. Very helpful were they in hemming and fringing the blue and gold badges provided for graduates, non-graduates, trustees, and guests. These satin ribbon badges, of three devices, were alike in bearing the seminary seal and name, and the semi-centennial dates, while those for graduates bore the class year also.

Outside preparations were efficiently carried on under the direction of Mr. Porter, the steward, whose executive ability proved equal to the demand of unnumbered details, expected and unexpected. In due time the unusual sound of hammer and saw echoed through the seminary grounds, when to the settees and benches scattered about in shady spots were added long rows of new seats in the grove; and tables were made under the lawn-party trees,— for was not the weather sure to be fine on Thursday, the day for lunch-box collation?

Over by the observatory, the caterer, Mr. Legein of Springfield, pitched his spacious tent and set up his culinary establishment. Near the old Dwight house was the tent for registration, where coaches were to leave their loads and where a bevy of "middlers," instructed in advance, were to aid the teachers in charge in keeping record of arrivals and in distributing the badge, tickets, programmes and other information to which each guest was entitled. On another side of the tent one stand was devoted to the delivery of the Memorandum catalogues; another to the sale of the seminary History; a third to the sale of whitewood goods engraved with views of the seminary buildings. On the wide lawn between the registration tent and the library, with Williston hall in its rear, was the tent for audience, two hundred feet by fifty, with seats for over two thousand. Tiers rising from the platform on three sides were made for the students of 1887; for the faculty, trustees, and special guests, provision was made in the rear of the speaker's desk; leaving the main area for former students and the general public. The names and mottoes of the different classes were suspended over this area to invite the alumnæ of those years to come together beneath. The rear of the tent behind the platform was adorned with the seminary motto: "That our daughters may be as cornerstones polished after the similitude of a palace." The tent was decorated with bunting in the national colors, and on the tent poles were shields bearing the state and national coats of arms, and words of welcome.

About the grounds large head-lights were placed on stands, here and there, to furnish illumination for the promenade concert and reception of Wednesday and

Thursday evenings. Chinese lanterns and colored lights were in readiness to decorate the buildings and the grove.

Outside the seminary grounds the Village Improvement Society continued and extended improvements begun by private enterprise, attended to streets, street lighting, sidewalks, shade trees, the village green, and to the general beautifying of surroundings.

Decoration of the village church for the Sabbath and for Wednesday was assumed by members of the class of '88.

By Saturday the High School building was fitted up for a dormitory, room for seventy-five beds having been made by the removal of desks and seats. Rows of white cots gave the seminary gymnasium also the look of a hospital ward.

As far as it could be, the usual work of anniversary week was done in advance. So many found it practicable to pack and send home a trunk no longer needed that many loads were taken away before guests began to arrive.

A few friends came on Saturday, including two former principals, Mrs. Mary Chapin Pease, 1850–1865, and Miss Ward, 1872–1883. Mrs. Helen French Gulliver, principal from 1867 to 1872, had come early in the term, and given aid in planning and arranging details. Among others welcomed early was Mrs. Martha Scott Dickinson, a teacher from '45 to '55.

JUBILEE WEEK.

SUNDAY.—The public exercises of Jubilee week began under clear skies with the baccalaureate sermon Sabbath morning by Rev. Dr. Laurie, who was pastor of the village church at the time of Miss Lyon's death. His appreciation of her spirit and work appeared in the sentence, "Not Mt. Holyoke Seminary made prominent through connection with the kingdom of Christ, but the kingdom served by Mt. Holyoke Seminary." No other standard was held before the forty-seven seniors sitting together in front of the great congregation, than that of the text, "All things were made by Him and for Him."—Col. 1 : 16.

At three in the afternoon Dr. Laurie met the "Mount Holyoke Missionary Association" of students, and gave them counsel and encouragement drawn from his own missionary experience. Miss Martha J. Chamberlain of '53, and Miss Helen Norton of '63, both from the Hawaiian Islands, were also present and spoke.

MONDAY AND TUESDAY.—The public examinations of the week closed Tuesday noon with that of the seniors in moral science. Final preparations completed, the first floor of the main building was thrown open, and the afternoon was spent in receiving the welcome throng of arrivals, whose plans for the week were in no wise changed by the ominous south wind, or the gathering clouds that grew thicker and heavier every hour. The registration books closed the night before with fifty names; that night with three hundred and sixty. Letters declining invitations came from many leading educators because the graduating exercises of their own institutions interfered. The evening was given to an informal reception and an exchange of greetings between long separated friends. Married names were quite forgotten; gray-haired " girls " called each other by the old names, to the amusement and wonder of the children and even grandchildren who were present. The husbands who came were in some danger of being temporarily forgotten. Though a few were said to "wander about in a desolate and abstracted manner" most of them shared in the general enthusiasm, and some one suggested that their place on this great occasion of rejoicing was to be the " Jubilee Hims."

WEDNESDAY AND THURSDAY.—Wednesday morning the village presented a scene of unusual activity. Alumnæ were hastening to and fro for breakfast, and singly or in groups from the restaurant to the seminary, where class meetings began at 8.30. In private parlors or public rooms, in Williston hall, seminary hall, or dining room, laboratory, library or reading room, up stairs or down stairs, a well advertised meeting-place had been assigned to each of the fifty classes and every one knew where to find her classmates. All the fifty years were represented, and every senior class except the first; not till the last moment was the hope abandoned that Mrs. Persis Woods Curtis, the only surviving graduate of '38, would be able to come and with Mrs. Cowles to lead the procession of alumnæ.

The public exercises of the morning were to be in charge of the present and former principals of the seminary. Five of the seven who have been at its head were present. The two deceased were represented by their associates, Miss Lyon by Mrs. Eunice Caldwell Cowles, and Miss Whitman by Mrs. Sophia Hazen Stoddard. Mrs. Cowles was the one to aid Miss Lyon at the opening of the seminary in 1837, and Mrs. Stoddard not only helped Miss Whitman in carrying it on when its failure was confidently predicted at Miss Lyon's death, but at a later day stood at the helm herself.

Class meetings were only continued, not closed, by the summons to fall into line, for it took much time to join, in the order of their classes, all parts of the procession of nearly fourteen hundred women, including the present students, three hundred and fifteen in number. As at the twenty-fifth anniversary, "there were no teachers that day" —or, rather, none but Mrs. Cowles.

It had been the tradition for fifty years that rain never fell on the anniversary procession. And this one on Wednesday had similar exemption on its way to church, though clouds hung low and showers fell before and afterward.

That day was given to the alumnæ; the morning to a general reunion, the afternoon to the annual meeting of the National Association, and the evening to an alumnæ reception, where two thousand in all are said to have been present, notwithstanding the pouring rain.

The semi-centennial and graduating exercises of Thursday were followed by after-dinner speeches, and by the usual senior reception in the evening.

MOUNT HOLYOKE SEMI-CENTENNIAL.

The following extracts are from an account of Wednesday and Thursday in *The Congregationalist* of June 30, written by Miss Dyer of the editorial staff, who was present.

This is the real queen's jubilee, is the idea that constantly impressed itself upon a thoughtful observer. Not Victoria upon her throne, but Mary Lyon regnant in the hearts and lives of more than three thousand pupils is the queen to whom America bows the knee and offers more than royal honor. Only a few impressions and a mere outline of the picture can be given.

Outwardly the scene was full of bustle and novelty. Every house in the neighborhood was crowded with guests, and many lodged in South Hadley Falls and Holyoke. Everything was planned with wonderful system. Nothing seems to have been forgotten that was necessary to a guest's comfort. The bountiful and beautiful hospitality of the affair was one of its chief charms. Everybody was welcome. Everybody felt at home. There was a constant procession of vehicles to and from the seminary,—private carriages, hacks, barges, stages,—each filled to its utmost capacity, besides an endless number of express wagons laden with supplies, and drays groaning under a weight of trunks. People poured in from nearly every state in the Union, from Europe, Asia, Africa, and the Sandwich Islands, one graduate from the Hawaiian kingdom leaving behind her four children and nineteen grandchildren! The final registration of students reached about eleven hundred, to which were added several hundred guests, many of them husbands of the alumnæ. It was decidedly interesting to examine this record of names. They were strangely familiar; scarcely one that had not appeared in print as teacher, missionary, leader in church and benevolent work, or wife of pastor or college professor. Several were old and valued contributors to our own columns. What is still more remarkable, not a single year of the entire half-century was unrepresented either by teacher or student.

Wednesday was Alumnæ Day. And what a day! What pen can do the subject justice? Early in the morning there was a stir of eager expectancy about the building as the different classes, in the order of their graduation, formed in procession to march to the church, the present pupils bringing up the rear. Classmates who had not met for perhaps twenty, thirty, or forty years, exclaimed with delight, and called each other by their given names, on finding that neither silvered hair, nor widow's garb, nor any of time's outward marks, had changed them beyond recognition. In many cases both mothers and daughters were represented in their respective classes. Slowly the procession filed down the familiar steps, across the spacious lawn, past the snow white tents, to the village church. The edifice was filled to overflowing and camp chairs were placed in the aisles. Has this earth ever witnessed such a gathering of elect women?

On the platform sat the honored principals, Miss Blanchard and Miss Edwards, showing no sign that heart and brain had been taxed to the utmost in preparation for the occasion, but rejoicing with all their hearts that they had lived to see this day. By their side sat their predecessors in office, Mrs. Mary Chapin Pease; Mrs. Sophia Hazen Stoddard, who presided with that simple dignity which seems to mark the bearing of every woman upon whom Mary Lyon ever left her impress; Mrs. Helen French Gulliver and Miss Julia E. Ward; also Mrs. Eunice Caldwell Cowles, Miss Lyon's first associate. After a brief but singularly fitting address of welcome from Miss Blanchard, singing, and prayer, Mrs. Cowles came forward as the most direct representative of the founder of the school. Her appearance was the signal for such a round of hearty and affectionate applause that her eyes kindled with a new brilliancy, and a flush of pleased surprise crept over the delicate features whose beauty no age can dim. For more than half an hour she entertained her listeners with reminiscences of Miss Lyon, and at one point, when she gave that inimitable "Good morning, young ladies," the entire assembly rose to their feet with an enthusiasm which could not be restrained, amid clapping of hands and waving of handkerchiefs. "Tell me what it was like," asked one of the secretaries of the American Board, who heard of the scene. As well ask me to paint a sunrise on Mount Rhigi as to formulate in words the posture, the rare smile, the inflection, the *personality* of that greeting.

"Speak to the daughters of Holyoke that they go forward," was the message that Mrs. Cowles gave as best expressing the sentiment of Miss Lyon, could her voice be heard out of the heavens to-day.

Among the interesting facts presented in a paper prepared by Mrs. Pease and read by her daughter, was a statement that more than one-fifth of the women in the employ of the American Board have been connected with this institution, and that of two thousand who have been teachers, about one hundred taught twenty-five years or more. A poem by Miss Julia H. May, principal of the May School in Strong, Me., a very pleasing address by Mrs. Ann Webster Eaton of the class of '42, and a paper on "Early Teachers" by Mrs. Burdette Hart of '46. were other good things at this memorable feast. A report from Mrs. Gulliver announced that $28,000 had been raised for the Mary Lyon fund.

Mrs. Moses Smith, president of the National Alumnæ Association, presided with her usual efficiency at the alumnæ meeting in the afternoon, and also read an able paper on "The Future of the Seminary." Then came a series of poems, papers, and addresses, largely reminiscent in character, greetings from a dozen or more alumnæ associations, each so full of wit and wisdom that it seems invidious to mention one without saying something of all. But a passing allusion, at least, must be made to the tender words of Mrs. Mills of Brooklyn, California, who told the story of her mother's wish, and its fulfillment, for her six daughters, who were all trained at Mt. Holyoke, their life there—studying and teaching—covering a period of twenty-five years; to the humorous paper of Miss Charlotte Morrill, and to that of Miss Ellen C. Parsons formerly of the Constantinople Home, who revived the hallowed associations connected with Mt. Holyoke's "Sacred Hours."

The rain, which had been falling at intervals all day, settled down the latter part of the afternoon into a persistent pour, and interfered with the illuminations and promenade concert on the grounds in the evening. But the front balconies were decorated with Chinese lanterns, and the Florence band discoursed sweet music, while within all was light and cheer and happiness. Governor Ames and some of his staff were present, also two of the seminary's most generous donors, Mr. E. A. Goodnow of Worcester, and Mr. A. L. Williston of Northampton.

Again, on Thursday morning, the rains descended and the floods came and beat upon the tent where the exercises were to be held. It was an unprecedented event. For fifty years the sun had shone upon Mt. Holyoke's anniversary day, and what else could be expected on this grand occasion? It was an exceedingly wet rain! The ground was soaked, the mud was inches deep, pools of water stood in the roads, and what could be done? What, indeed, but to go forward in the spirit of one of Holyoke's daughters who went south soon after the war, to take charge of a school for colored youth. When her life was threatened unless she left the place, she coolly replied: "I am going to stay here till I die, and, if possible, make a success of this school. You may shoot me if you wish, but I do not intend to leave." In like manner many waters could not quench, neither could floods drown, the purpose to celebrate this semi-centennial. Trustees and faculty, seniors, students, and guests, marched serenely to their places beneath the dripping canopy. What was the procession from Buckingham Palace to Westminster Abbey compared with this! Gentlemen sat in overcoats and ladies in waterproofs, with an appearance of taking joyfully the spoiling of their goods. The roof, secure enough in any ordinary weather, leaked in places, but umbrellas were calmly spread. Forty-seven seniors, with a heroism that Joan of Arc might have envied, quietly folded away their white dresses and appeared with smiling faces in ordinary attire. Prayers were offered, joyful anthems were sung, President Tyler's admirable address was read, diplomas were presented by President Seelye in his most felicitous manner, and yet scarcely a word was heard by the majority of that vast audience of two thousand or more persons. Even those on the platform, unless very near the speakers, could not hear because of the noise of the elements. Noon approached and the question of rations became a practical one. It was easier to sit there hungry than to venture forth in such a drenching rain to the restaurant tent or to the seminary dining hall. Still, nobody seemed disturbed. There was perfect confidence that Mt. Holyoke Seminary was equal to any emergency. And it was. At the proper time, Mr. S. E. Bridgman, that indefatigable trustee, announced that no one need move from his seat, as lunch would be served without delay. Lunch? Where was it coming from? Was the miracle of the loaves and fishes to be repeated? Presently a force of colored waiters appeared, laden with white pasteboard boxes in which was a dainty lunch of sandwiches, cake, and fruit, followed by cups of delicious coffee and lemonade. When was it prepared? Much of it during the silent hours of night, when the weary guests were wrapped in slumber.

In a city with markets close at hand, this may have been easy enough, but in a country town, whose resources seemed already taxed to the utmost, it appeared little short of a miracle.

There is no denying that the rain was really a grievous disappointment, but the spirit in which it was received served to illustrate, in a marked manner, the *esprit* of the seminary in all its teachings and traditions. It was a great deal to miss hearing the lively sallies of Hon. Henry D. Hyde of Boston, who presided over the afternoon exercises, and to lose the earnest words of such speakers as Dr. N. G. Clark; Miss Freeman, president of Wellesley College; Miss Evans, principal of Lake Erie Seminary; Prof. Millingen of Constantinople; Prof. H. M. Tyler of Smith College, and others, but the disappointment was somewhat relieved by knowing that the addresses are printed in a special issue of the Springfield *Republican*.

MISSIONARY MEETING.

Thursday morning's procession, hidden under umbrellas and waterproofs, was watched from the seminary windows by many whom prudence forbade to encounter the storm, even for the short distance to the tent. Some of these "shut ins" were returned missionaries, to whom, chatting together in separate circles, there came, from a suggestion of Mrs. Rhea (Sarah J. Foster, '55), a unanimous desire for "a thanksgiving meeting,—and in the seminary hall, where the faces of Mary Lyon, Fidelia Fiske, and others look down in perpetual benediction and inspiration; that at this Bethel they might review the way in which God had led them, and worship him with praises." The bell was rung, a few messengers went through parlors and halls, and a large number was soon assembled. Taking her seat at the piano, Mrs. Bowen (Flora P. Stearns, '69) started the hymn "From Greenland's icy mountains," and the familiar strains brought others to the hall. Some say there were three hundred there before the meeting closed. Mrs. Rhea, joined by Miss Shattuck, the only one of the present faculty that ever saw Miss Lyon, invited missionaries and missionaries' mothers to the platform. Among them were Miss Fritcher, '57, from twenty-four years in Turkey; Miss Rice of '46, Miss Fiske's associate, for twenty-two years in

Persia; and Mrs. Rowell (Malvina Chapin of '41), for forty-four years in the Hawaiian Islands, the oldest foreign missionary present. The first to leave the seminary for work abroad,—Charlotte Bailey of '38,—who left before the end of the first year to go to the Zulus as the wife of Rev. Aldin Grout, was kept by the rain that day at her present home in Springfield. Of those who have been engaged in teaching and home missionary work from the end of the same year until now, one was present—Miss Sarah Mather, from St. Augustine, Florida.

Prayer was offered by Mrs. Abbie Goulding Kumler of '55; Miss M. A. Chamberlain of '53, from Honolulu, read the second Psalm, and Mrs. Rhea struck " the key-note of royalty and loyalty, the highest and divinest note of heaven or earth, especially from Jehovah's own words in the sixth verse, 'Yet have I set my *King* upon my holy hill of Zion;' and from the eighth verse, words appropriate among the hills and mountains of this locality, and of this mount of privilege;" and continued:—

> The two mountains suggest two other mountains on which may *alma mater* abide forever: Pisgah, overlooking the world promised to Christ; and Hermon, with the transfigured Christ. Behold the need and the supply. From such a vision and revelation, above all other blessings let us ask for *alma mater* entering on her second half-century, the baptism of missions, that more and more her daughters, chosen and polished, may carry the gospel to the ends of the earth; and may this be the distinguishing mark and the highest glory of the Mary Lyon College until the millennium.

As this was an impromptu occasion, each missionary was desired to speak simply as a representative of the heathen women for whom she had labored. Mrs. Rowell spoke of the power of the gospel among Hawaiian women; Miss Fritcher of the joy of laboring twenty-four years among the girls and women of Marsovan; and her classmate, Mrs. Kate Pond Williams, of the work in the Constantinople Home.

Mrs. Blakely (Gertrude Sykes of '53), whose daughter is in Turkey, said: " The best thing is to have the love of God in our own hearts; the next best is to communicate it to others, and, if we cannot go ourselves, to send our daughters."

Mrs. Rhea in the same vein told of her own and her daughter's joy in the return of the latter to Persia, the land of her birth. Miss Sarah Dorr of '58, from Cambridge, having obtained leave to speak, gave a brief but glowing account of Mrs. Rhea's own missionary life, alluding to the memoir, " The Tennesseean in Persia."

A granddaughter of the seminary, Mrs. Frances Hazen Gates of '75, daughter of Mrs. Martha Chapin Hazen of '42, spoke of the fondness of heathen women for ornaments. When they ask why missionaries do not wear them, she replies that the chief ornament of a Christian woman is a meek and quiet spirit. As the heathen women bear the mark of their god in their foreheads, so should Christian women reflect the image of their Master.

Mrs. Bowen alluded to the beautiful Smyrna rugs we see, and asked that admiration for the work should be joined with prayer for the women who painfully but patiently weave them, carrying the patterns in their minds.

Missionaries in the field were fervently and tenderly remembered in prayer by Miss Chamberlain.

Mrs. Alice Gordon Gulick of '67, from Spain, referred to the danger of an ocean voyage amid fogs and icebergs, and to a captain who, when asked after two nights on the bridge without sleep, how he endured it, replied, " This is what I was made for." " What am I made for?" should be the question of each Christian.

Miss Helen S. Norton of '63 bespoke interest in the daughters of Hawaii, and dwelt on the need of increased interest in the foreign work in general; illustrating the insincerity of those who plead interest in the home-field for lack of interest in the foreign, by the instance of a Chinaman who, though within reach of such a laborer, was three years in this country without hearing that there is a God.

The following, from an appeal by Miss Grace E. Wilder of '83, though prepared for the alumnæ meeting, is inserted here:—

Dear friends, we may be doing good, but is it our best? Are we pointing to lesser lights while we might be guiding souls to *the* Light? "The good is a great enemy of the best." Mary Lyon left her good work at Ipswich to do a better; be satisfied with nothing less than your best. Do you ask, "Am I called?" God's scheme of service is as wide as his scheme of salvation. "Whosoever will may come." "Let him that heareth, say come." If Christ's desire to save souls is measured by the sufferings and death of Calvary, his desire to have us soul-winners is measured by the same. Yet, just as he would have us seek him with the whole heart before we find him, so he would hear from our lips the earnest cry, "Lord, here am I, send me," before he grants the gift of service. Let not Satan delude us with the thought, "If God wants you to be a missionary, he will make you one," but let us, rather, crave the privilege and power of leading souls from "darkness to light." In a world tenanted with 800,000,000 heathen, Christ's work for us is surely very direct soul-work. Can we doubt it while at every tick of that watch four souls pass from this world without a knowledge of salvation? Can we let a feeling of unworthiness or fear of hardship, or a waiting for some special call, keep us from the expression of love Christ asks us to give by obeying his last command?

O that the girls of '87 might not leave these halls to-day, without the definite purpose to do his bidding! This chart, representing 511,000,000 of heathen and Mohammedan women and girls, calls us to the work left for us to do. What stronger call could we have than the fact that these, many of whom can be reached only by women, are living "without Christ, without God, without hope in the world!" The privilege of enlisting in this work is ours, not because of our fitness to do it, but because Jesus has said, "All power is given unto me in heaven and in earth, go ye therefore."

Mrs. Helen French Gulliver of '57, representing the Woman's Board of Missions, made an appeal for missionary teachers, now much needed.

Mrs. Rhea then urged upon those in the audience who are officers of missionary boards to consider the great wisdom of Christ in sending laborers two and two, and added:—

A young girl in her teens with the ink of her diploma scarcely dry, and without experience of life, goes out to the foreign field and is sometimes speedily overwhelmed, breaks down, and returns home a failure and a wreck. The best way to prevent such a calamity is never to send one alone. "But the funds will not allow two," you say. Then have more funds and send two. "Perhaps the work requires only one." Then enlarge the work and send two. Let us settle this matter by past experience of suffering and failure, and especially by the example of Christ, never to be improved upon. Let the girls in a school like this, friends and congenial, be united for life in tender and loving ties of sympathy, unselfishness, and helpfulness; let them be set apart by the church and the Holy Ghost; and then let them have their own home in comfort and dignity, and their work together in the mission station. And if they set out to be happy and useful thus in the Lord's work, nobody in the world has a better chance. They will be happy. I know from experience. My own happy life, though in widowhood, with Miss Rice in Persia confirms it, and I can recommend such a union. *Alma mater*, give us missionaries, two and two!

Grateful mention was frequently made of indebtedness to the seminary for missionary interest, with fervent desires that it may be a source whence laborers shall never be sought in vain.

Rev. Allen Hazen, D. D., from India, after speaking earnestly of the great work and the honor of having part in it, offered the closing prayer and pronounced the benediction.

In writing of the occasion afterward, Mrs. Rhea said:—

No description can do justice to the freshness and brightness of the speeches, perhaps just because they were so unpremeditated. Every one began *in medias res* and spoke out of her heart and to the point, and some very eloquently. If it were worth while to wish, I might wish that the girls could have been there to catch the fire. I so wanted them, not theirs, that we had in sweet welcome, friendly courtesies, kind, unwearied, self-denying service; oh how beautiful they appeared, like real members of the family in a home entertaining their mother's elderly and honored guests! They impressed me very favorably in all things, and I would like to thank them as well as the teachers who made the occasion so pleasant. But I wanted them for missions. Pairs of loving hearts, Christ-serving, cultured, winning, Holyoke-trained Fidelia Fiskes and Mary Susan Rices, to teach and preach the gospel to the heathen, giving up all things and finding all things, "an hundred fold in this life and in the world to come life everlasting." With holy avarice and inflamed heart I looked and loved and coveted those girls for missions.

PROGRAMME.

SUNDAY, JUNE 19.

10.30 A. M., VILLAGE CHURCH.—Baccalaureate Sermon,
Rev. Thomas Laurie, D. D., Providence, R. I.

MONDAY, JUNE 20.

2.15 P. M., { SEMINARY HALL, WILLISTON HALL, } Anniversary Examinations.

8 P. M., LECTURE ROOM.—Recess Meeting,
Led by Miss L. W. Shattuck of '51.

TUESDAY, JUNE 21.

0.15 A. M., { SEMINARY HALL, WILLISTON HALL, } Anniversary Examinations.

AFTERNOON AND EVENING.—Welcome of Arrivals.

WEDNESDAY, JUNE 22.

8.30 A. M.—Class Meetings.

10 A. M., VILLAGE CHURCH.—General Alumnæ Meeting :—
Song of Welcome, written by Miss Bruce, '87.
Address of Welcome by Miss Blanchard, the Principal.
Poem in response, Mrs. Park, '62, Athens, Pa.
Address, Mrs. Cowles, Assistant Principal 1837-38.
"Work of the Alumnæ," Mrs. Pease, Principal 1850-65.
"Medical Work of the Alumnæ," Elizabeth L. Peck, M. D., '76.
"At Home," Mrs. Goodwin, '71, Center Harbor, N. H.
Report on Mary Lyon Fund, Mrs. Gulliver, Principal 1867-72.

Solo, Mrs. Holmes, Instructor in Music 1862-66.
"A Reminiscence," Miss May, '56, Strong, Me.
"Our First Things at the Seminary, Mrs. Eaton, '42, Palmyra, N. Y.
Sonnet, "To the Mothers," Mrs. Blake, '84, Mansfield Valley, Pa.
"Early Teachers," Mrs. Hart, '46, New Haven, Conn.
Trio, "O Memory."
"Early Trustees," Mrs. Stow, '59.
"Prominence of Science," Miss Shattuck, '51, Senior Instructor.
"The Stone of Scone," Mrs. Candee, '58, Lowell.
"Reminiscences," Mrs. Carter, '71, Boonton, N. J.

LETTERS FROM

Miss Jessup, '47, Associate Principal 1855-62.
Miss Ellis, '55, Associate Principal 1867-72.
Miss Peabody, '48, Principal Western Seminary, Oxford, O.

2 P. M., VILLAGE CHURCH.—Annual Meeting of Alumnæ Association:—
Reports from Officers.
Reports from Branch Associations.
"Reminiscences," Miss Morrill, '61, Brooklyn, N. Y.
"The Old and the New," Mrs. Severance, '58, Manchester, Vt.
Solo, "One sweetly solemn thought," Miss Paine, '86.
"Sacred Hours," Miss Parsons, '63, New York City.
Hymn, Mrs. Gamwell, '61, Westfield.
"The Future of the Seminary," Mrs. Moses Smith, '58, Detroit, Mich.
Discussion of Resolutions.

7.30 P. M., SEMINARY HALL AND PARLORS.—Reception to Alumnæ.
7.30 TO 9.30, ON THE GROUNDS.—Concert by the Florence Band.

THURSDAY, JUNE 23.
9.30 A. M., IN THE TENT.
Anniversary and Graduating Exercises:—
Historical Address, Rev. Wm. S. Tyler, D. D., LL. D., Amherst.
Jubilee Hymn, Rev. S. F. Smith, D. D.
Presentation of Diplomas, Pres. J. H. Seelye, D. D., LL. D., of
Amherst College.
Intermission.

AFTER-DINNER SPEECHES FROM

Rev. N. G. Clark, D. D., LL. D., Boston.
Miss Freeman, President of Wellesley College.
Rev. Mr. Harding, Longmeadow.
Miss Evans, Principal of Lake Erie Seminary.
Prof. Millingen of Robert College, Constantinople.
Miss Edwards, Associate Principal.
Mrs. Moses Smith, '58, Detroit, Mich.
Prof. H. M. Tyler of Smith College.

EVENING—SEMINARY HALL AND PARLORS.
Reception to Graduating Class.

NOTE.—Parts of the Programme for Wednesday were omitted for want of time. Such papers are inserted in their places with the stenographer's report which follows.

BACCALAUREATE SERMON.

BY REV. THOMAS LAURIE, D. D., PROVIDENCE, R. I.

VILLAGE CHURCH, Sunday, June 19, 10.30 A. M.

"All things were made by him and for him."—Colossians 1 : 16.

IF these words were the utterance of mere poetic fancy, they might be beautiful but forever remain only a dream. If they merely gave expression to human desire, all good men might unite in it, but there could be no assurance that the desire would ever be fulfilled. Yet, as the utterance of a man who spake as he was moved by the Holy Spirit, they are not only full of glory, but infinitely trustworthy.

The evangelist tells us, "He was in the beginning with God." Not, "He began to exist," for as the creator he knew no beginning, but all else is the work of his hands. We go out under these bright skies of June, and the springing grass, the opening flower, each leaf and blossom, are all from him. So, too, is the light, and every vital force in nature. Nor these alone, but in heaven there is neither glory of place nor inhabitants but declareth his handiwork. The spiritual bodies of those inhabitants, their mental powers, their moral excellence, are all from him. Then, not only were all made by Christ, but all were created for Christ, and that is a truth which, the more we apprehend, the more we are filled with joy unspeakable; for its glory reaches back through the eternity before creation. Before any matter existed from which this globe was to be formed, God purposed that it should exist for Christ. Before anything was created to occupy that globe, God purposed that it, also, should exist for Christ, and as each in continuance was fashioned it was consecrated to his glory. And what is that glory? No mere splendor of external form, but the greater splendor of his undertaking, and so all was consecrated to the promotion of his work as the Saviour of the world, and that means the perfect deliverance of the earth from sin. It means that there has been and is one who is almighty and omnipresent to stand up for truth and right in all places, and work out human well-being through all the ages. One who is never discouraged by difficulty and who never makes a mistake. Can righteousness be driven from such a world, or our race perish with such a friend?

Viewed in this light, creation from the first must have seemed glorious. True, there was the place where Adam would sin, but near by was the place where the deliverer would first be made known. Here was the place where God would meet with Abraham, and there the temple would be glorified with the presence of the Son of man. There, too, was the place for each of his works of power and words of grace; here he would meet the woman of Canaan, there he would raise Lazarus, and yonder would stand his cross. Nor did Palestine monopolize this grace; on that maritime plain Paul would be born, by that roadside he would be converted, and from that distant Italian locality he would ascend to heaven. This inland town in Germany would produce Martin Luther, and in that other he would stand alone against Rome,— and yet not alone, for Christ is in him and round about him. Time would fail me to tell of scenes to be made glorious by Wickliffe and Latimer, Calvin and Knox, Baxter and Bunyan, Whitefield and Wesley, to say nothing of men now living or yet to be born. Here in our own Connecticut valley would be the birthplace and field of labor of Jonathan Edwards. Yon large monument of Mary Lyon, filled with those there training to serve her Saviour, and on the other side of that mountain the grave of David Brainard. And what shall I say of the scenes of the labors of other missionaries the world over? And then, more numerous than the sands upon the shore, the sons and daughters of the Lord Almighty who consecrate by their service and their prayers the whole world to Christ. There is no spot so cursed by sin that shall not be more blessed by the grace there revealed, so that where sin hath abounded, grace shall much more abound. The idea of converting the whole earth to Christ is grand, but it rests on the grander idea of a world created for Christ, nor could it otherwise be realized. The power of such a creation moves with omnipotent energy from age to age, till the whole plan of God with all its blessed results shall stand forth complete.

See its foot-prints across the centuries. In spite of the destroyer in Eden, there is the seed of the woman crushing the serpent's head. Though the adversary fills the earth with pollution and violence, there is the Son of man washing it all away in the deluge,—type of a better cleansing equally commensurate with the race. And when, after that, even his chosen people propose to go back to Egypt and to bondage, God comforts himself with looking at the future of a world which had been created for Christ, saying, "As I live, all the earth shall be filled with the glory of the Lord."

Listen to another breaking forth of this same joy of God. "The nations rage, the peoples imagine a vain thing, the kings of the earth set themselves, and the rulers take counsel together against the Lord and against his Christ." He that sitteth in the heavens laughs and repeats the decree, "The Lord said unto me, Thou art my son. Ask of me and I will give thee the nations for thine inheritance and the uttermost parts of the earth for thy possession." Behold the fruit of creating this world for Christ! and it is as certain to ripen as that God lives and has power to do his will in the army of heaven and among the inhabitants of the earth.

It may seem as if all this went for nothing when Israel became the most selfish of the nations, but for two thousand nine hundred years a remnant was offering this prayer: "God be merciful unto us, and bless us, and cause his face to shine upon us." Why?—"That thy way may be known upon earth, thy saving health among all nations. Let the peoples praise thee, O God; let all the peoples praise thee. O let the nations be glad and sing for joy." Israel might forget that prayer, but God never forgets that this world was made for Christ.

If the psalmist was so emphatic, the prophets were not less outspoken. Through one the Lord saith, "Look unto me and be ye saved, all the ends of the earth," and to Zion he saith: "Arise! shine! for the glory of the Lord is risen upon thee, and nations shall come to thy light." Not, they shall wait for the light to come to them, but they themselves come to the light. "Yea, many nations shall come, saying, Let us go up to the mountain of the Lord and he will teach us of his ways, and we will walk in his paths."

The Son of God thus speaks of himself through the same prophet: "It is too light a thing that thou shouldest be my servant to raise up the tribes of Jacob; I will also give thee for a light to the Gentiles, that thou mayest be my salvation unto the end of the earth," and that word spoken two thousand six hundred years ago shall not pass till every jot and tittle of it be fulfilled.

Need I remind you that visions seen in Babylon and Susa embraced the history of Greece and Rome, or how grandly Daniel foretold that "the greatness of the kingdom under the whole heaven should be given to the saints of the Most High, whose kingdom is an everlasting kingdom?" Was it accident that caused these words to be engraved over the lofty portal of a temple in Damascus, after it had been changed into a church? Centuries after, when it is again changed into a mosque, Moslems cover the words with plaster and deem them blotted out forever, but the rains of over a millennium have washed out the plaster, and again the grand ascription, "Thy kingdom, O Christ, is an everlasting kingdom and all dominions shall serve and obey thee," looks forth, silently awaiting its fulfillment; for earth was made for Christ, and with God one day is as a thousand years and a thousand years as one day.

But more than all else we want to know the mind of the man Christ Jesus. This theme was much in his thoughts and out of the abundance of the heart the mouth spake. Does he describe the field of his operations? "The field," he says, "is the world." And he looks on his angels as already sent by him to gather out of his kingdom all that causes stumbling.—Do not intoxicating drinks cause stumbling?

Even while he restores sight to the blind his thoughts are reaching far out and he saith, "I am the light of the world." Does he speak of himself as the living bread which came down from heaven? He saith, "The bread of God is he who cometh down from heaven and giveth life unto the world," and again, "The bread that I will give is my flesh, which I will give for the life of the world." Yea, so full is his heart of this truth, that it finds expression in other forms. "I lay down my life for the sheep, and other sheep I have, which are not of this fold; them also I must bring, and they shall hear my voice, and there shall be one flock and one shepherd." You see he is looking forward to the time when the whole earth shall constitute his flock. And in his most sacred communion with the Father he saith, "As thou hast sent me into the world even so have I also sent them into the world," and is importunate that the world may believe; and in another place, "That the world may know that thou hast sent me."

Even Satan when he sees how Christ though then the leader of only a few disciples aspires to the possession of the whole earth, finding that other motives have no power to move him, makes the exhibition of all its kingdoms and the glory of them the basis of his temptation to sin. But our Lord, while abating no jot of desire for the salvation of the race, seeks it only in the appointed way of suffering obedience.

Nor is his view of the future all brightness, like the views of some in our day, but as King of kings he tells the Pharisees, "The kingdom of God shall be taken from you and given to a nation bringing forth the fruits thereof," and then as if he saw the scenes of the judgment rise up before him,—"He that falleth on this stone shall be broken in pieces: but on whomsoever it shall fall, it will scatter him as dust." A recent railroad disaster is described as reducing massive cars to splinters, but Christ speaks of human bodies reduced to a cloud of dust, and Christ is the truth, he never exaggerates.

His point of view is one that belongs to him alone, as he says: "All authority in heaven and on earth hath been given unto me. Go ye, therefore, into all the world and preach the gospel to every creature." Yea, he is bold to say to every preacher in lands and ages furthest apart, not,—"I will hurry from one to another as fast as possible," but, as if it were even then being fulfilled, "Lo, I am with you alway, even unto the end of the world, my presence with you in all lands moves on that broad line down through the ages." Again he says, "This gospel of the kingdom shall be preached in the whole world for a testimony to all the nations and then shall the end come," and as if that end were present before him, he saith: "When the Son of man shall come in his glory, and all the angels with him, then shall he sit on the throne of his glory, and before him shall be gathered all the nations."—See how he keeps in view the whole area of his kingdom,— "and he shall separate them one from another as the shepherd separateth the sheep from the goats." Not, as some fondly dream, the power of his presence transforming the wicked into the righteous, as alchemists dreamed of transmuting baser metals into gold, but his presence, like a consuming fire, separates between gold and dross,—and yet his own words are always the best if we could only appreciate their force, as one does on the east of the Jordan, when in early morning he sees myriads of sheep pouring out from a city gate in one undistinguishable mass. How can these flocks ever be separated? is his inward thought. And even while he asks the question one shepherd utters a call, and instantly there is a movement in all parts of the mass. Another and another calls, each his own, and long lines radiate in response from a common center till each flock follows its own shepherd separately to its own pasture. So in that coming day the word of Christ shall separate the righteous from the wicked and each company go to its own place.

This foresight of Christ takes in individuals as perfectly as if each one existed alone. So he said of her who anointed him in the house of Simon, "Verily I say unto you, wheresoever this gospel shall be preached in the whole world that also that this woman hath done shall be told for a memorial of her."

The great trouble is that we lose sight of this glorious Lord of lords and struggle through the fight as if each fought by himself, instead of constituting one army with Christ for our leader. How does he teach us to look out on the battle? Not as a series of disconnected skirmishes occurring at random, but each fitting perfectly into the other and each contributing to the victory of all according to the plan of Christ.

So he prays, "Glorify thy Son, that the Son may glorify thee, even as thou gavest him authority over all flesh, that whatsoever thou hast given him, to them he should give eternal life." And in this way the interests of truth and right are taken up into the interests of this Son of God. Wonderful arrangement of our Father in heaven! Were God to deal with us on the basis of our deserts, we must perish. But God so arranges that to glorify his Son is to bless us with all spiritual blessings, and doing for us exceeding abundantly above our thoughts, is rewarding that beloved Son. This is a far better salvation than else had been our portion, for it unites us to God in a way that I dare not describe save in his own words, "I in them, and thou in me, that they may be perfected into one; that the world may know that thou didst send me, and lovedst them, even as thou lovedst me." Then our union with Christ is such that the love of the Father to his own Son becomes love to us, and that Son prays, "That the love wherewith thou lovedst me may be in them, and I in them." Therefore, as sure as we are in Christ he is in us, and the love of God to us is identical with love to his beloved Son. Surely we have here Christ's own exposition of that expression, "Joint heirs with Christ."

But it may be said this is mere theory, for after all these same joint heirs with Christ are very imperfect. True, in us it doth not yet appear what we shall be, or, if it does, it only appears in part. But *in him* even now it appears complete, and that which he is in himself tells what shall be the issue of his grace in us, for we shall be like him when we shall see him as he is. Himself, then, is the pattern to which he is even now conforming us, nor will he stop until he changes even this body of our humiliation into the likeness of the body of his glory.

So much for individuals, but how about the world which was created for him? Here I advance no private speculations. I only point you to his own command, "Pray after this manner,—Thy will be done on earth as it is in heaven," not, "pray that all may hear of Christ," for many hear, and never believe. Not, "Pray that all may enter the church," for many are in the church who are not Christ-like, but that on earth sinners may do the will of God as angels do his commandments in heaven. Do you ask, Can that ever be? Rather put the question, Is anything too hard for the Lord? but you say, No progress is made. That is not so sure. The kingdom of God deals with things unseen. Then the work is thorough. Western towns may grow up in a night, and they disappear as quickly, the structures are so flimsy; but the pyramids of Egypt were not built so rapidly. And remember earth was made for Christ, and he has undertaken to save it, and to this end he has all power on earth and in heaven. Yea, more than undertaking it, he is doing it right before our eyes; and did he tell us to count the cost before we begin to build, without himself counting the cost before he began? If he did not hold back from the cost of the garden and the cross, we need have no further anxiety. I know the church is not yet perfectly conformed to Christ. I also know that it is more like him to-day than ever before. The standard of character is higher, and it still goes up. The standard of Christian character is higher, and still goes up. There are churches in New England in which Christians worship to-day for building which lotteries were authorized by New England legislatures. Could that be repeated now? Slaves once toiled in New England as well as in the South, and where is slavery to-day? Dueling was once common among us. Is it now? Deacons once got their living on Puritan soil by selling rum. Could one of them repeat the experiment to-day? I have conversed with men who remembered the time when a prayer-meeting was unknown in the city of Boston. Need I ask how it is to-day? There are men now living who can look back to the time when there was no missionary society in the land, neither home nor foreign. Two years ago the missionary societies in the United States expended in one year $2,127,657. It is not very long since a church could be counted evangelical, and yet make no effort to bring men to Christ, but that also is being buried along with the want of interest in missions; and outside the church, the saloon approaches the edge of the same grave and must go in. So Christ takes possession of the home-land, in spite of the incoming tides of popery, infidelity, anarchy, and Mormonism. And abroad, while the area of Christendom enlarges, that of heathendom dwindles daily. Compare the India of 1800 with the India of 1887; the Japan of 1850 with the Japan of the present; central Africa ten years ago with the central Africa of to-day that already reports revivals on the Congo. All these things betoken progress, but they are only the dawn of the morning, while the sun that "shall no more go down" has yet to climb to its meridian. Wait till you, also, after passing through the gate of pearl, shall see in the light of heaven that joy set before Christ when he endured the cross. And as you gaze on it forever, you will see whether it is worth all the trials through which God now leads his church to its possession, yea, whether it is not worthy to be the reward even for the sufferings and death of the Son of God.

On ordinary occasions I might apply this subject to those who refuse Christ, and bid them see who it is whom they refuse. To-day in the light of the history of this seminary just placed in your hands, see the part to which God has called it in bringing this world back to Christ.*
Nor is there presumption in this, for still, as of old, God chooses the weak things of the world to put to shame the things that are strong. When Christ formed that secluded hillside in Buckland he saw the part

---

* Out of two hundred and sixty-one women now in the employ of the American Board of Commissioners for Foreign Missions abroad, fifty-six were pupils of Mt. Holyoke Seminary, or one in five of the whole number.   T. L.

assigned it in the promotion of his kingdom. Sixty years ago men saw opposite yonder cemetery only a huckleberry pasture, but from the beginning Christ saw not only all that has yet taken place on that favored spot, but all that is yet to take place there, or to flow from it to the ends of the earth. Mary Lyon and Fidelia Fiske, one representing the work done here, the other the streams of salvation that flow hence to distant lands—Mary Lyon and Fidelia Fiske are not puffed up to-day with a sense of their personal importance, they do not feel that God was dependent on their labors, but as they see how God has been pleased to link in this seminary with the advance of his kingdom they praise his grace, and the more they appreciate this grace the more humbly do they cry, "Not unto us, not unto us, but unto thy name give glory." They take pleasure in this anniversary only so far as we are in sympathy with their desire to see the Lord alone exalted. Not Mount Holyoke Seminary made prominent through connection with the kingdom, but, the kingdom served by Mount Holyoke Seminary, is their way of putting things. So far as we sing in that key, our voices are in tune with theirs. Time forbids to dwell on the great principles brought to light in the history of this seminary, nor is it needful, for during the week they will receive ample vindication from abler hands.

But let all whose feet have stood within these sacred walls thank God for the privilege. I have never been a member of the seminary, but I have never approached it during these forty years without inhaling the fragrance of a field which the Lord hath blessed. It is like the ointment which another Mary poured on the feet of Jesus, fragrant with the aroma which he gave it at first, but more fragrant from association with himself. It is the home of holy thoughts, a center of fellowship with Christ. Prayer is the language of its inmates, and of all other prayer that which is made for him continually that he may see of the travail of his soul and be satisfied. It is easy to preach in a place where the truth finds such hospitable welcome, where the heart so fills with it that it must needs flow forth in words. It is a New England Bethany where Christ enjoys to-day the sympathy he once found with Mary and her sister and Lazarus. This seminary has chosen that good part which shall not be taken away from it.

As for you who have dwelt under its roof, the anointing which ye have there received from him abideth in you, and shall abide. You cannot unlearn what you have learned there of fellowship with Christ, nor would you unlearn it if you could. Other schools may exalt literature, you, have here grown into oneness with Christ in loving and saving a world, and death so far from breaking off that growth will only make it perfect. Sometimes in Massachusetts Bay ships battle with the wintry storms till they are literally encased in ice. Then they turn toward the Gulf stream and though at first there is no change, yet soon, without touching a rope, or changing a sail, the ice disappears from hull and rigging, and instead of Arctic cold is welcome warmth. So may you who have here turned from the cold selfishness of earth into living communion with the Saviour of the world, continue along the same line till in heaven you join those who have gone before, in perfect sympathy with a heaven whose inhabitants are gathered from every tribe and tongue and people and nation, for there also his servants shall serve him, and as in heaven Christ completes the work begun on earth, so his disciples are still co-workers with him, enjoying there the full fruition of the work with which they identified themselves here, even the blessed work of leading to Christ the world that was created for him at the beginning.

GENERAL MEETING OF THE ALUMNÆ.

VILLAGE CHURCH, 10 A. M., Wednesday, June 22.

MRS. SOPHIA HAZEN STODDARD, Acting Principal 1865–67, presided. Singing of the doxology was followed by a responsive reading conducted by Miss Edwards, Associate Principal:—

1. My soul doth magnify the Lord.
2. My spirit hath rejoiced in God my Saviour.
1. For he that is mighty hath done to me great things;
2. And holy is his name.
1. Bless the Lord, O my soul,
2. And all that is within me, bless his holy name.
1. Return unto thy rest, O my soul,
2. For the Lord hath dealt bountifully with thee.
1. What shall I render unto the Lord
2. For all his benefits towards me?
1. I will take the cup of salvation,
2. And call upon the name of the Lord.
1. I will pay my vows unto the Lord,
2. Now, in the presence of all his people.
1. Bless the Lord, O my soul,
2. And all that is within me, bless his holy name.

Prayer was offered by Mrs. J. P. E. Kumler (Abbie C. D. Goulding, '55). A song of welcome, written by Harriet L. Bruce of '87, was sung by the Seminary quartette. A brief address of welcome was given by Miss Blanchard, the Principal:—

It gives us great pleasure to welcome you all here to-day, and to tell you that your very coming is a benediction. It will be a still greater pleasure to greet you one by one, and to look into the faces not only of those whom we have personally known, but into those also of the earlier alumnæ, with whom we feel scarcely less acquainted, so much have we heard and thought of you.

Though you miss the face of the sainted one who gave many of you your first welcome here, and to whom each of us would turn most eagerly were she here to-day to repeat that greeting welling up from her great heart of love, we cannot help thinking that she is here, that she rejoices in all our joy, and that she says, just as she did fifty years ago, "My soul doth magnify the Lord."

You remember how she said when about to lay down her work, "I should love to be permitted to come back and watch over this seminary, but God will care for it." And surely God has cared for it.

We are glad that you are here to-day to help us make mention of the ways in which he has faithfully fulfilled the expectations that he kindled in her heart, and to tell us anew of her aspirations and of her large desires for the daughters of our land and of the world.

We bid you welcome, also, who came in later days and who entered into a larger fulfillment of her plans. You, too, have received the impress of her spirit, and have felt the value of her work. And so it is to us all a day of jubilee.

Your letters have mentioned your joyful anticipations in the thought of "coming home," and of meeting old-time friends. May all those anticipations be more than realized!

In the name of *alma mater*, cordially we welcome home the daughters of Holyoke!

POEM IN RESPONSE.

MRS. D. T. PARK, ATHENS, PA. (Lydia M. Carner, '62).

O, *alma mater*, well beloved,
 What joy to hear thy welcome call!
What joy to gather once again
 Within thy blessed prayer-built wall!

O, friends, sweet friends of old, who come
 From far and near, from o'er the sea,—
How blest in fair Jerusalem
 To keep this feast of jubilee!

Ye who have wandered long and far,
 O, see ye not what God hath done?
The *alma mater* ye once knew
 Hath fairer, broader, richer grown.

How have her borders been enlarged
 By those who gave with lavish heart!
How have her treasures been enriched
 By gifts of nature, science, art!

We look with happy, tear-dimmed eyes,
 Upon her bright prosperity,—
Upon her thousand daughters come
 To keep this joyous jubilee.

We think with tender wistfulness
 Of all the absent ones to-day,
Whose loving, longing hearts said "Go,"
 While duty sadly bade them "Stay."

ALUMNÆ MEETING.

May we not think, O sisters dear,
   That still another, happier band,
Of those whose wand'rings all are o'er,
   With us to-day in spirit stand ?

Can you not see the joyous throng
   Whose prayers have all been turned to praise,
With benedictions on their brows,
   And heavenly lovelight in their gaze ?

Our hearts are full, but we'll not weep,
   " With courage and with faith " we'll pray;
For prayers of fifty years ago
   Are being answered here to-day.

Across the waters, England keeps,
   With stately pomp, her jubilee,
For fifty years of queenly rule
   Of Her Most Gracious Majesty.

A woman rare and true and good,
   Unrivaled sits upon the throne;
No other with such noble heart
   Hath worn proud England's jeweled crown.

Her name is like a household word
   Where'er her loyal subjects dwell;
And all her gentle, kindly deeds,
   The children weary not to tell.

The cannons boom,—the people shout,
   And high triumphal arches twine,
And march rejoicing through the land
   Whereon the sun doth always shine.

And from the prisons of the realm
   The wretched captives are set free,
To swell the voices of the throngs
   That keep Victoria's Jubilee.

Doth not the saintly one who prayed
   In faith, who lived and loved and taught,
Wear better than an England's crown,
   Gemmed with the stars for which she wrought ?

She sits enthroned, a very queen,
   In hearts she drew with gentle plea
Out of the prison house of sin,
   To Christ whose love had made them free.

Her name is, too, a household word—
  A power that reaches wide and far;
Her words of wisdom echo yet,
  Wherever Holyoke's daughters are.

She walketh now the golden streets,
  And naught her gladness ever mars;
For many turned to righteousness
  She shineth ever as the stars.

In gratitude we pause beside
  This "golden milestone" in our path,
And from the sweet fields of the past
  We gather precious aftermath.

We meet with smiles and clasp of hands,
  And waves of rapture lave the heart;
But thoughts of sadness crest the waves—
  An hour of joy, and then we part.

Sweet friends, the recompense will come,
  Beyond life's turbid, restless sea,
When in the New Jerusalem
  We keep eternal jubilee.

ADDRESS OF MRS. J. P. COWLES OF IPSWICH.

(Miss CALDWELL) Associate Principal, 1837–38.

I THANK you for this greeting and I bespeak your patience, for patience you will probably need before I am through. This is a wonderful occasion for me, and I have many things to say, for I may never have another opportunity. All the year the friends have been kindly inviting me to be here to-day, but I have been ill and did not think I could come, and sent word that I could not, and that that must be final, but Miss Edwards wrote me the most eloquent letter that I ever received in my life, urging me to come. My husband never wrote me one half so eloquent. The motive Miss Edwards presented was a very strange one. She wanted me to represent Miss Lyon! It reminded me of what some one wrote at Niagara more than fifty years ago: "I have seen a candle—I have seen the sun; I have seen thy picture—I have seen thee, O Niagara." I am but a candle to the sun with whom I was associated. But I thank you all for your greeting and for your welcome.

Perhaps you do not know that a great deal of the planning of this seminary was done at Amherst, in the house of Professor Hitchcock. The first time I was there I went with Miss Lyon on this very business of founding the seminary. Strange, but she always took me with her. She used to like to talk to me even if I did not reply. That house held some of the largest hearts in the world. I cannot see how this seminary could have come into existence without their aid. It was much to have the pecuniary aid of Deacon Safford and Deacon Porter, men then comparatively unknown. Professor Hitchcock, not President then, in the very prime of life, had been all over Massachusetts to prepare a report of the geology of the state for the General Court. The first night that we spent at Mr. Hitchcock's the floor of the guest chamber was covered with geological specimens. We had to tread gingerly not to step on them as we went to our bed; and the house was just as full of good, large-hearted benevolence and kindness. I think it was a great deal for Mrs. Hitchcock to take us in, with all her cares, and little Edward, an infant in her arms.

Even in those days Miss Lyon used to talk about the wonderful time there would be fifty years hence when we should come to celebrate the founding of the school. It lived in her mind before they had decided to give her the little help they did, as much as it lives here now, and she used to say sometimes, "I don't believe but you will be in it." I said I should be old and feeble, nothing but a fossil, but she said, "No, you will be just the same as you are now." Very kind in her, you know. I am sure she rejoices and is glad to-day to see these troops of ladies who have come up here to render her honor due. It is high triumph for her.

Will you allow me to say, as her mouthpiece, "Good morning, young ladies!" [Said in a tone so like Miss Lyon's that the whole audience rose to their feet simultaneously and with great enthusiasm.]

I want to say now just what I think she would say were she here. I am sure she would be glad that the impress of good sense and of holiness, in the old sense of wholeness, pervades every part and parcel of this school still. The impress she made on it has someway come down, and I find it in these halls just as it used to be. I find just such girls, such wonders to me, loving, unselfish, determined to go forth and do good as the Lord gives them opportunity, ready and willing to engage in his work. She is glad that that stamp remains; for she is the same that she was when she went away. She is glad that Christ is still the head of the school, the great Shepherd looking after this flock as a whole and as individuals; that he comes here and sups with these dear girls, just as he used to come and sup with us fifty years ago.

I think I may say she is very glad indeed that the under shepherds of this flock are still ladies; that the trustees and persons in power have been able to find ladies capable of directing the studies, the impulses, and the hunger of these young women, the daughters committed to their charge. I think she would agree with me in wondering why,—if at the beginning, the first attempt at a female college ever made, a woman was fit to be the head of it,—why after all this planting of colleges there should not be college-educated women fitted to stand at the head of a college. It does seem as suitable that a woman should stand at the head here as that a man should stand at the head of a college for young men. Really I cannot see why a man should be put over this college any more than a woman over Amherst or Williams.

Again, she is glad of anything that advances womanhood. She is very glad to know that the trustees have found three women on whom they have ventured to confer trusteeship. And I think I can almost see her coming and putting her soft, white hand on Mrs. Gulliver and Miss Blanchard and Mrs. Williston and saying: "I know you will be true to your trusts. It is a step in the right direction, perhaps other steps will be taken on the same road."

There is another thing. She is glad of every advance that is made here in science, in the knowledge of language and in literature and in general history. She placed this seminary at the very front of schools for women. Ipswich had been, but she put it fully up with Ipswich, and then Ipswich declined. Miss Grant used to say, "I must decrease but she will increase." I remember the letter in which she said this. Miss Lyon kept the school where she put it. She did not stand still. There was never a woman more constant in change. She was like the sun, moon, and stars, always going forward, forward, forward. Miss Grant, her superior in some respects, used to almost find fault with her because she moved so fast that she did not always keep the track; but she never got very far away. Though constant in change, she was always progressive. If she found she had made a mistake she stepped back very quickly, but she usually made the right step the first time. This seminary can make no step in advance that she would not make if she were here. She rejoices in every advance that is made. I want to speak to the daughters of Holyoke that they go forward. I bring that as her message. I have a fashion of waking up with a text in my mind that seems to be an answer to the prayer with which I went to sleep. That was the text that came to my mind the next morning after receiving Miss Edwards' letter: "Speak to the daughters of Holyoke that they go forward!" Keep the school in the front rank. Do not be stationary. Move as fast as anybody. If you are not at the head, then get to the head.

Again, there was nothing on which Mary Lyon was so set as on educating persons of small means. She used to say, "We don't want to build for the rich, and we cannot build for the poor, but we can build for the middle class who have moderate means and large aspirations;" and it was for that class that this school was founded. If the rich girls come, let them come and welcome, and I warrant they will not find so much fault as some who are not rich. But when they come don't bow down to them; treat them well but don't act as if you felt below them or above them. This American fashion of bowing down to a big house, a big man, a big purse, is absurd. I have been delighted that thus far the school has been kept within such limits that girls of moderate means can attend. When we began, the expense was sixty dollars a year. Miss Lyon used to say that a girl of energy and ability could secure that. There was one man who wanted to have scholarships, but she said: "No, I want to have them all on the same level, to come with their own money. If a girl is worth educating she will contrive to get the sixty dollars and the extras; she will earn it, or borrow it, or will find an uncle or some one who will give it to her." She was very decided not to have any fund. I think the ladies have done nobly in carrying out this plan. Miss Lyon is very glad that you are, however, attempting to raise a fund (and she is willing enough to have it in her name) to keep expenses where they are now. The salaries of the teachers then were two hundred dollars—and I think I had one hundred dollars of hers. Some of you teachers worked for less than two hundred dollars. It would be impossible with the great band of teachers necessary to carry forward science and literature as they ought to be carried on, to be now properly paid at sixty dollars a year from the scholars. You do not want to live as we lived that first year, though we did not any of us suffer. I am delighted to know that the Mary Lyon fund is growing every day, but I want it to grow to a hundred thousand dollars. I know that she is glad of every dollar that comes to endow this institution. I remember that some fifteen years ago Mrs. Julia Tolman (who was one to hold up the hands of Miss Chapin), when she came to die, left a fund of four thousand dollars, the interest of which should be appropriated to giving needed rest to weary teachers. And I can but think that when Miss Lyon saw Miss Tolman she expressed to her her gratitude that she remembered the worn and weary teachers. This is very little, but what if it should be the nucleus of a fund like that of another institution that sends a teacher away once in seven years for a year's rest? If you should raise such a fund do not fear that it will not be welcome. The alumnæ of this school are not rich and some of them have a hard time of it, but I think you have all had happy lives. You look like happy women. You have had some sorrow with the happiness; you have had the bitter with the sweet; we all have. But some of you have rich husbands, and some husbands that will give largely themselves will not give to their wives to give, though others will, so I hope you will carry this matter on your hearts. Suggest to those who have money that they give to this school. You may bring more with your tongue than others do with a full purse. Don't be afraid to send a little. Don't be ashamed to send a dollar; send a prayer with it. The influence of the two mites has been going on ever since they were thrown into the treasury. A dollar may be more for you than a thousand to some one else. But give that dollar.

I come to another question. What do I think Miss Lyon would say about calling this a college? Well, I think that Miss Lyon would not care much whether it was called a seminary or a college. I do not think she would consider it a matter of any great consequence. If the scholars want to have it a college, and that is the fashion, let them do as they like. But I think she would say: "Be sure and have it a college before you call it so. If the girls want a degree, why it is natural; I don't know but I should like to have had one. I guess we would better let them have it." I remember very well what she said once about having girls classed. The first time girls were ever classed, as boys are in college, was in Derry, N. H., when Miss Lyon was with Miss Grant. The first diploma ever given to a woman was in Derry, and she entirely approved. To me such things were extremely indifferent. I asked her why she cared to have these classes. She said that the girls came to school longer and thus got a better education if there was a prospect of a diploma.

But if you call it a college, have it a college. The name Mount Holyoke was a compromise. I have spoken of Miss Lyon's being at Amherst. In those days Professor Hitchcock wrote a series of articles for a Boston paper in which he suggested that it should be designated "The Pangynaskian Seminary," because it was to educate the woman all through. They were to have domestic, intellectual, moral, and religious culture. The friends of the undertaking feared that this suggestion would kill the school. But it struck the community. Even yet, once in a while, I find an old man who asks about the "Pangynaskian." The very name called the attention of the Massachusetts people to the school more than any other one thing, though of course such a cumbrous name was not adopted. Professor Hitchcock was never afraid of anything under the sun that was true. The papers would not print Miss Lyon's articles unless she paid for them line by line, but Professor Hitchcock was a man of such influence that they would publish his papers on this Pangynaskian Seminary. Everybody laughed at the name, and that set them to talking about the school, and I do not suppose that it diverted a dollar, nor a cent. The question then arose what it should be called, and finally they fixed on Mount Holyoke. And now you like "college" better than "seminary." If you change the name, why not call it the Mary Lyon College? It will save one embarrassment—you will get rid of the "Female." I always write the name with a remonstrance. A seminary has no sex. When you are considering a name will you not consider this? The doctors tell me I may live for six or eight years yet. If I should live to hear that this was the Mary Lyon College, I think I should sing, "Praise God, from whom all blessings flow."

Mrs. Mary W. Chapin Pease, after a few words of greeting, introduced her daughter, Hattie R. Pease, a member of the class of 1886, who read for her the following paper:—

THE ALUMNÆ AT WORK.

It has been justly said of the daughters of our *alma mater*, that, "They are a mighty force in all good work." They are prominent in every department of benevolent and philanthropic effort, both as workers in the field and as managers of the work at home. With them "the field is the world." They are found to-day as missionary laborers in Japan, China, Burma, Ceylon, India, Syria, Persia, Turkey, Spain, Africa, South America, and the Islands of the Pacific. The American Board Almanac for 1887 reports two hundred and sixty-one missionary women as now in its service. Fifty-six of these, more than one-fifth of the whole number, are Holyoke women. Four others are under appointment by the Woman's Board of Missions, one from each of the classes, '85, '86, and '87, and one from '62. To these may be added twenty-five or more in the employ of other missionary societies, and also the teachers in the Huguenot schools in South Africa, who, though not connected with any missionary society, were called to do missionary work, and responded in a missionary spirit.

Some of these missionary friends have for a long time been laborers in the foreign field. Of those who have been thus engaged for thirty years or more, we can name :—

Mrs. Charlotte Bailey Grout, Natal, South Africa.
Mrs. Susan Reed Howland, Oodooville, Ceylon.
Mrs. Martha Sawyer Burnell, Madura, India.
Mrs. Maria K. Whitney Pogue, Honolulu, H. I.
Mrs. Malvina J. Chapin Rowell, Waimea, H. I.
Mrs. Hannah Maria Condit Eddy, Beirut, Syria.
Mrs. Eunice B. Day Bliss, Constantinople, Turkey.
Mrs. Alzina V. Pixley Rood, Natal, South Africa.
Mrs. Elizabeth A. Smith Noyes, Pulney Hills, India.
Mrs. Abby T. Linsley Wilder, Natal, South Africa.
Mrs. Lucy E. Stearns Hartwell, Foochow, China.
Mrs. Susan A. Brookings Wheeler, Harpoot, Turkey.
Mrs. Ann E. Clark Gulick, now in Okayama, Japan.
Mrs. Louisa Healy Pixley, Natal, South Africa.
Mrs. Caroline R. Wheeler Allen, Harpoot, Turkey.

More than twenty others have been in the work between twenty and thirty years, and about the same number between fifteen and twenty years. Twenty-one have been called from a shorter term here to the higher service above.

In the various departments of benevolent effort in the home land, the women of Holyoke have been abundant in labor. A large number have been employed in the Home Missionary field. Mission work in our cities and large towns has enlisted the sympathy and aid of many. In the twenty years since the colored race at the South was freed from servitude and the army of teachers with spelling book and Bible entered the field, numbers of Holyoke pupils have been among the foremost workers. For instance, five of the ten unmarried lady teachers in Fisk University are graduates of the seminary. Among the Indians, Chinese, and Mormons, also, they have labored with excellent success. Into the temperance work, under the auspices of the Woman's Christian Temperance Union, and similar organizations; into prison reforms, flower missions, orphan asylums, industrial schools,—into every sphere of labor for the fallen and the unfortunate, they have entered zealously, manifesting the spirit of the Saviour's precept, "Freely ye have received, freely give."

In executive offices the ability and efficiency of Holyoke alumnæ have been abundantly tested. They are found everywhere as directors and as workers in woman's missionary boards, and in the various departments of philanthropic work. For instance, one vice-president of the Woman's Board of Missions in Boston, who is also on the editorial committee of *Life and Light,* seven presidents, eleven vice-presidents, and eleven secretaries of Branches are Holyoke women. So are the president, five vice-presidents, and four of the executive committee of the Woman's Board of Missions of the Interior, and several of the presidents, vice-presidents, and secretaries of the State Branches. In the Woman's Presbyterian Board of Missions of the Northwest, the president, three vice-presidents, one foreign secretary, one of the executive committee, and seven presbyterial presidents are also Holyoke alumnæ. A little incident in connection with one of the annual meetings of this Board illustrates this point. Mrs. H., at that time president of the Board, unwittingly named, as a committee for the nomination of officers, Mrs. M. of Milwaukee, Wis., Mrs. R. of Lake Forest, Ill., and Mrs. K. of Cincinnati, O. This called Mrs. R. to her feet, with the remark, " Mrs. H. must have Holyoke designs on this Board, for the three ladies named are graduates of Mt. Holyoke Seminary, and classmates."

We also find Holyoke women in the following and many other similar positions : matron, for seventeen years, of Deaf and Dumb Institute, Washington, D. C.; matron, for sixteen years, of Chicago Home for the Friendless; principal, for seventeen years, of Orphan Asylum, Brooklyn, N. Y.; president of National Association for the Relief of Colored Women and Children, Washington, D. C.; president of Bureau of Employment to supply needy women with work at their homes; leader in city missionary work, Hartford, Ct., and member of State Board of Charities; member of New York State Board of Charities; manager of Brooklyn Seaside Home for Children ; in charge of Home for the Children of Missionaries ; national superintendent of Sunday-school temperance work of Woman's Christian Temperance Union ; prominent officers in state branches of Woman's Christian Temperance Union.

As teachers, many of the alumnæ have filled places of prominence and responsibility. From a long list that might be given we name the following :—

The Principal, for fifteen years, of Adams Academy, Derry, N. H.
The Principal, for ten years, of Ladies' Department, Kimball Union Academy, Meriden, N. H.
The Principal, for nineteen years, of Wendall Institute and May School, Strong, Me.
Two Principals of Abbot Academy, Andover.
The first President of Wellesley College, Wellesley.
The Principal of Dana Hall Preparatory School, Wellesley.
The Principal, for thirty years, of High School, Westboro.
The Principal, for twenty-three years, of High School, Easthampton.
The Principal, for twenty-one years, of Oak Street Primary School, Springfield.
The Founder and, for thirty-one years, Principal of Oak Hill Seminary, West Haven, Ct.
The Principal, for twenty years, of Young Ladies' Institute, Windsor, Ct.
The Principal, for seven years, of Young Ladies' Boarding School, Stamford, Ct.
The Founder and, for twenty-five years, Principal of American Kindergarten, New York City.

ALUMNÆ MEETING. 41

The Lady Principal, for twenty-four years, of Brooklyn Heights Seminary, Brooklyn, N. Y.
The Lady Principal of Rutger's College, New York City.
The Principal, for fifteen years, of St. Agnes' School, Albany, N. Y.
The Principal, for eleven years, of Chatham Academy, Chatham, N. Y.
The Principal, for eleven years, of Neversink Seminary, Port Jervis, N. Y.
The Founder and, for twenty-two years, Principal of Houghton Seminary, Clinton, N. Y.
The Associate-Principal, for seventeen years, of Temple Grove Seminary, Saratoga Springs, N. Y.
The Principal, for twenty-one years, of Oak St. Grammar School, Buffalo, N. Y.
The Founder and, for thirty years, Vice-Principal of Mountain Seminary, Birmingham, Pa.
The Principal, for thirty-one years, of Arch Street School for Young Ladies, Philadelphia, Pa.
The Principal of Normal Kindergarten Training School, Philadelphia, Pa.
The Principal, for sixteen years, of Ivy Hall Seminary, Bridgeton, N. J.
The Principal of Normal Department of Howard University, Washington, D. C.
The Founder, and Principal for eighteen years, of Fairfax Hall Boarding School, Winchester, Va.
The Founder, and Principal for thirty-three years, of Cleveland Academy, Cleveland, O.
The Founder, and Principal for seven years, of Willoughby Seminary, Willoughby, O.
The Principal, for nineteen years, of Lake Erie Seminary, Painesville, O.
The Principal, for thirty-two years, of Western Female Seminary, Oxford, O.
The Principal, for eleven years, of Glendale Female College, Glendale, O.
The Principal, for fifteen years, of High School, Goshen, Ind.
The Principal of Ladies' Department of Wheaton College, Wheaton, Ill.
The Principal of Ladies' Department of Knox College, Galesburg, Ill.
The Principal of Ladies' Department of Lake Forest University, Lake Forest, Ill.
The Principal of Academic Department of Knox College, Galesburg, Ill.
The Principal, for twenty years, of Monticello Seminary, Godfrey, Ill.
The Principal, for fifteen years, of Normal Department of High School, Chicago, Ill.
The Founder and Principal of DuQuoin Female Seminary, DuQuoin, Ill.
The Principal, for twelve years, of Michigan Female Seminary, Kalamazoo, Mich.
The Principal, for four years, of Wisconsin Female College, Fox Lake, Wis.
The Principal, for eleven years, of Wisconsin State Normal School, Oshkosh, Wis.
The Principal of Albert Lea College, Albert Lea, Minn.
The Lady Principal, for four years, of Hillsdale College, Hillsdale, Mich.
The Lady Principal, for ten years, of Iowa College, Grinnell, Ia.
The Lady Principal of Whitman College, Walla Walla, W. T.
The Principal, for eleven years, of Primary Department of Oregon State University, Eugene City, Or.
The Principal, for eighteen years, of Rice Institute, Trinidad, Colo.
The first and second Principals of Cherokee Female Seminary, Tahlequah, Ind. Ter.
The Associate Founder and, for twenty years, Principal of Mills Seminary, Brooklyn, Cal.
The Principal of Field Seminary, Oakland, Cal.

The Founder and, for nineteen years, Principal of Armour Institute, Memphis, Tenn.
The Founder and, for twelve years, Principal of Mt. Hermon Seminary, Clinton, Miss.
The Principal, for thirty years, of High School and Girls' Department of Franklin Academy, Columbus, Miss.
The Principal, for twenty-six years, of Young Ladies' Seminary, Augusta, Ga.
The Principal of Normal Training School, Mendoza, South America.
The Principal of Sherbrooke Academy, Sherbrooke, Canada.
The Associate Principal of Demill College, Oshawa, Canada.
The Lady Principal of Oahu College, Honolulu, H. I.
The Principal of East Maui Seminary, Makawao, H. I.

We are sorry that we have not been able to learn the life record of every one of the 6,300 former pupils of the seminary before this Jubilee celebration, but time and strength have not allowed. We must, therefore, confine our summary of teachers to the members of the Memorandum Society, for of these we have definite knowledge. Of the 3,033 members, about one-half of all who have been pupils here, more than 2,000 have been teachers. More than 400 of these have taught between ten and twenty-five years; about one hundred, twenty-five years or more; and six, at least, have been thus engaged more than forty years. The years that these 2,000 members of the society have taught make an aggregate of over 13,000. It is as if seven persons who had been taught by Christ, and had been sent out by him to bless the world by imparting knowledge, had lived through all these years and had continued to teach for eighteen and a half centuries.

Not only in mission, benevolent, philanthropic, and teachers' work are Holyoke alumnæ occupied. Many other important positions are filled by them. As many as forty, representing twenty-four different years of seminary life, have become physicians, graduates of leading medical colleges in our own country or of renowned universities in Europe, successful in their practice, and enjoying the confidence of the communities where they are located.

One is vice-president of the Wisconsin State Teachers' Association. Another has for eighteen years been secretary of Adelphi Academy, Brooklyn, N. Y. Others are librarians of public and college libraries, school visitors, members of school boards, and the like.

Many have done excellent work in art and literature. Essentially workers in the world, they have written with such ability as to call forth strong expressions of commendation. Like the deeds of their hands, the products of their pens have had this controlling purpose, to do good. Many of them have been regular contributors to the press. They have written for nearly every standard religious and secular newspaper and magazine in the country. * * * * * Some have done editorial work. Others have written books. From a long list we select a few. One, of the class of 1863, a prominent temperance worker, is the author of "More than Conquerors," and other works. Another of the same class is the present editor of *Woman's Work for Woman*. One, of 1848, has written a history that has been adopted by the Canadian government for use in its public schools; she has also a series of interesting books for young people, which have been published both in this country and in England. One, of '52, has two series of books for children, ten volumes in each series; also, three or four other works, one of which, "William the Silent and the Netherland War," is a standard reference book in history. One, of '62, over the signature "Howe Benning," has written eleven books suited for Sunday-school libraries. One, whose name is held in loving remembrance by many school friends and fellow-teachers, for many years Bible reader and city missionary in New York, prepared tracts for use in her work, and also wrote two books, entitled, "Witnessing for Jesus in the Homes of the Lowly," and "Scenes in the Lives of the City Poor," "both of which give glimpses of her work, and on every page shadow forth her own Christ-like spirit." A memorial of Mrs. Banister is by one of the class of 1847. "Recollections of Mary Lyon," by Fidelia Fiske, is a work of much interest and particularly valuable for teachers. One, of '66, professor of German in Wellesley college, has translated "Ramona" into German, and has also rendered into English the work of a German author. One, of '64, is the author of a history of sculpture of acknowledged merit. Prof. Mather says of it, "We may remember with pride that with one exception (and that the work of a German author) the best history of sculpture ever written is by an American lady." Others have written interesting stories, school books that have been adopted by boards of education, translations from French and German, history, poetry, travels, works on art.

Of the 1,789 married members of our Memorandum Society, 432 have married clergymen, 153 physicians, 159 lawyers, and about 75 professional teachers.

When we speak of the alumnæ at work we do not forget the hundreds to whom Providence has assigned a quiet home life, who, in their daily round of cares and duties, making home attractive, training their little ones for a noble manhood and womanhood, are doing a work that angels might covet.

Some of the alumnæ, like our beloved Miss Jessup, have illustrated the Christian spirit by patient endurance of long years of suffering. "They also serve who only stand and wait."

We have taken only a very brief survey of the work of the Holyoke alumnæ. May it be that of each of us all the Master can at last say, "She hath done what she could "!

MEDICAL WORK OF THE ALUMNÆ.

ELIZABETH L. PECK, M. D., '76, SEMINARY PHYSICIAN.

THE work of Mt. Holyoke Seminary, varied and rich as it has been in many fields of labor, would scarcely be complete without mention of the medical study and practice undertaken by so large a number of its pupils.

The rise and progress of woman's medical education during the past half century stands out in relief amid other advances in her opportunities and training. This movement represents a struggle and aspiration later in time, it is true, but kindred to that which called forth the noble effort of our founder in the cause of woman's general education. It is one step out of what Canon Kingsley calls the "monastic idea of woman" toward her true place.

The school showed its progressive spirit by its early recognition of this opportunity for woman. Since 1860, when Dr. Mary Homer-Arnold first came, a lady physician has been resident here; and some of the pioneers in medical work have come from the ranks of its pupils.

Nearly forty Holyoke alumnæ are, or have been, engaged in medical work. Their professional studies have been pursued in nearly all the leading schools in America that admit women. Graduates of Ann Arbor, Woman's Medical College of Pennsylvania, Women's Medical College of the New York Infirmary, College of Physicians and Surgeons (Boston), and Boston University are among the number. Several have also studied at Zurich, Dresden, and Vienna.

Not only have a majority of these graduates had advantages for beginning the study of medicine fully equal to those enjoyed by the average medical student, but, desiring the most thorough preparation for so arduous a life work, many have secured for themselves the additional benefits of hospital experience, that invaluable introduction to the practice of medicine.

Their field of practice has been by no means a narrow one. We find them busy in all parts of our own land, and we have several representatives in foreign lands. Many of you know of the work of Dr. Holbrook in China, and of Dr. Kelsey—once resident physician here—in Japan. Dr. Fanny Wetmore is in her home in the Hawaiian Islands. Dr. Emerson-Morrow and Dr. Van Meter-Kelley are at work in Burma. Dr. Wadsworth-Bassian is practicing her profession in her Turkish home, while Dr. Andrews-Shepard is in Beirut, Syria.

Nor can we consider the field a narrow one in a professional sense. Naturally, the time and effort of medical women is directed toward the field of practice for which they are specially adapted and in which they are specially needed. But these women have not neglected to lay foundations both deep and broad; and it is in no spirit of narrow specialism that they have entered the realm of medicine.

Dr. Mary Smith, of Boston, after years of study, in America and in Europe, has been at the head of the New England Hospital for Women and Children, and is now a very successful surgeon in Boston; doing both general and gynecological surgery.

Dr. Charlotte W. Ford, formerly physician here, has a busy practice in Morristown, N. J.

Dr. Frissell, for eight years in Pittsfield, Mass., and the first lady practitioner there, is now settled in Springfield.

Dr. Gertrude Gooding, of Newport, R. I., after spending much time in hospital and dispensary work, is practicing homœopathy in Newport with success.

Dr. Ellinwood, and Dr. Marchant, who was here last year as seminary physician, have a large practice in Rome, N. Y.

Several of these physicians have married. Sometimes their active professional life has ceased with marriage; but Dr. Boardman-Pulsifer, of St. Louis, writes that though she has not practiced medicine, she has found time to use her knowledge, gained at home and abroad, in the work of training nurses for the sick.

Dr. Grace Peckham, who has published some articles in our journals, has received recognition as a worker in the field of nervous diseases.

Dr. Perry, of Taunton, and others, speak of the kind way in which they have been received by the gentlemen of the profession.

Among the younger alumnæ, several have recently finished their studies or are at present engaged in them. As an illustration of the thorough work done in our scientific department, we may speak of a member of the class of '86, who has been excused from one year of work in her medical course, on account of what she had done here in anatomy and chemistry.

Of our resident physicians, Dr. Emily Belden-McCabe, well remembered by those here between '64 and '68 as a woman of special talent, has recently finished her work. Drs. Breed-Welch, Mary Everett, Etta W. Payne, A. A. Richardson, and E. Callendar are also among those whose life work is done.

As we turn this page in the records of the work done by the daughters of *alma mater*, we are glad to see that, like that done by others of her children, it bears the character of her own—it is patient, progressive, practical—an earnest work for humanity.

AT HOME.

Mrs. EMERY A. GOODWIN, Center Harbor, N. H.
(Helen J. Angell, '71.)

Our mother calls her daughters home
   To crown her year of jubilee;
From distant continents we come,
   And from the isles of every sea;
From mountain heights, from desert sands,
From city streets and lonely lands.

We come, but some have come unseen,
   So closely cling the little hands,
So frail the lives that on us lean,
   So long the paths from foreign strands,
So large the work, so weak the frame;
But we in heart are here the same.

Our founder never knew how blest
   Her name, her work, her life, should be,
Could she come back from her sweet rest
   And sit with us beneath the tree
Whose germ she planted, she would cry,
"The Lord hath done this! What am I?"

And gazing on her pictured face
   Recall we all the blessed host
Whose home was once this hallowed place;
   Our buried treasures—not our lost.
O that the stone for this one day
From every grave might roll away!

That both the living and the dead
   At once might stand within these walls,
Where like the dew on Hermon's head
   The Spirit's gentle presence falls;
Where souls are clothed with heavenly might
To win in every earthly fight.

Dear *alma mater!* in God's hand
   Thy future lies; for us a day
Of meeting, by no parting spanned,
   Where God shall wipe our tears away;
For after night comes morning blest,
And after toil his perfect rest.

REPORT ON THE MARY LYON FUND.

Since Mrs. Gulliver, as one of the trustees, would be engaged in their meeting in the afternoon, her report as chairman of the committee on the Mary Lyon fund was given at this time.

Mrs. Gulliver.—I do not propose to make a formal report, for the fund will speak for itself. But you may like to know something of its history.

In the annual alumnæ meeting two years ago, looking forward to this "day of days," the request was made that the alumnæ should unite in a thank-offering to commemorate the day. A member of the Boston association proposed that a permanent fund should be secured for the support of the principal of the seminary. There was little discussion over it. It seemed eminently fitting that we should thus pepetuate the name of the noble woman to whom we owe so much. A committee was appointed from ladies present, a circular prepared and printed. The circulars were spread before the throne of grace. We asked that they might appeal to your hearts and be fruitful in bringing back aid in making this school what we wish it to become.

A treasurer, Miss Cowles, was appointed to receive the funds. She has been the source of a great deal of sunshine in the seminary for the past eighteen months. I will ask her to give you the report of the treasury.

Miss Cowles.—It gives me great pleasure to say that the fund of twenty thousand dollars is complete. And it gives me still greater pleasure to announce to you and to Mrs. Gulliver that the sum is still growing and that the amount in the treasury is now $28,150.

Mrs. Gulliver.—We thank each of you for taking this matter into your hearts as you have, and for your gifts. And we ask you to carry our thanks to all other contributors. Would you like to know how this result has been reached? The first gift to come was a check for $500 from Hartford, Connecticut. In our glad thanksgiving for this, we rejoiced also in the promise we saw in it of the helpful alumnæ association soon after formed in Hartford.

Then came a precious gift, which had started weeks before from far-off Kurdistan. You can imagine how we took those Bitlis sisters into our prayers that night and begged for God's blessing on their work.

For three months nearly every day brought us something. Sometimes it was but a dollar or two, but the spirit of loving loyalty in which it was sent made it of great value to us.

An unsigned note came one day containing the words, "The Rev. Roswell Hawks, the early friend and helper of Mary Lyon, has long since gone to his reward. The writer received personal favors and obligations at his hand, and in return sends the enclosed draft for $125, for the Mary Lyon fund, to be given in the name of Roswell Hawks."

Among other memorial gifts was $1,000 from a mother whose daughter, a student here thirty years ago, had just entered into rest.

From a graduate at the head of a flourishing seminary in the South came $100 with the message, "I send this money not as a gift but in part payment of what I owe to our beloved *alma mater*. May God's blessing go with it!"

Sometimes classmates united their gifts. The alumnæ associations responded loyally : New Haven, the oldest of them all ; the Northwest; Worcester; Philadelphia; Greenfield ; and Amherst, the latest formed.

The associations of the Hawaiian Islands and of the Pacific coast contributed. Sometimes for days no money would come, and we grew anxious. Then our treasurer would appear among us with a sunny face and we would learn she had been having communication with New York by way of 138 Montague street, Brooklyn. In addition to other generous gifts this association obtained $4,500 from the Marquand fund. The Boston association, having begun the work, did not fall behind any either in gifts or efforts.

In the name of the trustees, who aim to make this school all the strongest love can wish ; of the teachers, who are giving more to this work than any one outside can ever give ; of the students now and in all the years to come, whose advantages will be greater for what you have done and for what you propose to do,—we thank you all.

You have received from her beloved and honored co-worker Miss Lyon's message to the daughters of Holyoke. Will you " go forward "? The work of endowment is only begun. Shall we not soon have $100,000, of which $28,000 is already in the treasury? And then it must be followed by other hundreds of thousands, that the desires of sainted ones and of us all may be realized in the constant growth, the broadening and strengthening of this beloved institution.

As Mrs. Gulliver took her seat a telegram was handed Mrs. Stoddard, from Beloit, Wisconsin, bearing the love of Mrs. Susan Allen Blaisdell to her classmates of '47.

The solo, "O come, let us bow down," was sung by Mrs. Eliza Wilder Holmes, instructor in music, 1862-66.

ALUMNÆ MEETING.

A REMINISCENCE.

JULIA H. MAY, '56, STRONG, ME.

I WROTE some lines once on a time—
 'Twas thirty years ago—
And thought they were almost sublime,
 So little did I know.

Sprinkled with figures everywhere,
 And adjectives so sweet,
An anapest put here and there,
 And countless kinds of feet.

I copied them in letters clear,
 Correctly punctuated,
Then wrote, "Eight hours were used up here";
 And folded, labeled, dated,

I handed them to wise Miss Start
 Till they were criticised;
Her criticism cut my heart,—
 "Improperly capitalized."

But when she saw how deep it went,
 (The tell-tale crimson rose,)
She added, "Dear, I only meant
 'Twere better far in prose."

And so my lines I laid away,
 My sad, pathetic verse,
My blank, blank verse. But why to-day
 Their fancied wrongs rehearse?

My adjectives concealed by dust,
 My similes cremated,
My metaphors turned dark with rust,
 At length I graduated;

The prose of life began to read
 With mingled grief and pleasure;
And for long years I felt no need
 Of anapestic measure.

The years have slipped into the past;
 Gold hair is turning gray;
The girls are coming back at last
 The mothers of to-day.

And I am ordered to indite
  Another composition,
And let them see if it is right;
  I even have permission

To write a poem. 'Fifty-six!
  Let me your aid invoke,
For I am in a pretty fix,
  And fear it is a joke.

Will not the learned alumnæ
  Whose praise I should have prized
Look on and shake their heads at me,—
  " Improperly capitalized " ?

And if I air my musty rhymes
  And scent them *à la rose*,
Will they remember olden times
  And,—" Better far in prose " ?

Don't do it, girls! (Not you, sweet girls,
  The rosy, brown-haired lasses,
But those with silver in their curls,
  Who look at me through glasses.)

Forget the past imperfect deed,
  The blunder or mistake;
Forgive the scanty bearing seed,
  For *alma mater's* sake.

And if we've done one noble thing,
  Let us to-day aver,
We learned it underneath her wing,
  And owe a debt to her.

Oh, could each graduate turn to gold
  These treasured bits of knowledge,
How quickly would the world behold
  The Mary Lyon College!

Alumnæ! Classmates! Life's big book
  We've read, till each one knows,
Although poor thoughts sometimes may look
  Better far in prose,

There still are poems, gay or sad,
  Impressed on every page
Of life; youth's verses no more glad
  Than those of middle age.

Ah! when the school of life is done,
And through the twilight dim
Our Teacher calls us, one by one,
To read our rhymes to Him,

I think we shall not fear the call,
However incomplete
Our lines; to Him who knows it all
The good intent is sweet.

As June-day roses seem to grow
More bright each passing year,
And this dear spot has brightened so
Since last we studied here,

Brighter and better may it be
Unto perfection, even,
When budding earth for you and me
Has blossomed into heaven!

OUR FIRST THINGS AT MT. HOLYOKE SEMINARY.

MRS. HORACE EATON, PALMYRA, N. Y.
(Anna R. Webster, '42.)

OUR first entrance to the seminary was due to the purpose of a widowed mother. Her early trial in being unable to secure a higher education indicates that a school like Mt. Holyoke was a want, a necessity, felt by all the daughters of the land. When a young woman, she was most anxious to attend the school at Byfield, Mass., taught by Rev. Joseph Emerson, the instructor of Zilpah Grant and Mary Lyon. But her father had sent two boys to Dartmouth college, her mother spinning and weaving their garments from lambs of their own flock; he thought he could do no more. She then used all her eloquence with a wealthy neighbor to raise the money on loan, promising to teach on her return and refund with ten per cent. interest. A derisive laugh accompanied his reply,—" If a girl can read, write, and cipher as fur as the Rule of Three, 'tis all the eddication she needs." Through a long life, she could hardly allude to this disappointment, without tears. She influenced many young ladies of her town to become pupils of Miss Grant and Miss Lyon at Ipswich, Mass. All the teachers of our academy had to be from Ipswich.

She applied for our admission at South Hadley long before we could enter. At length the day came. To be in season for the opening, she took us in a one-horse chaise, on Saturday afternoon, eight miles to Concord, and then returned home. When the lengthening distance forbade another parting word, her right hand, raised for a moment and pointing upward, bade us look above.

We "rested on the Sabbath day, according to the commandment," and were off in the stage to Nashua at five o'clock on Monday morning. From Concord to South Hadley occupied the greater part of two days. The Granite State was then jubilant over its first railroad, hardly completed from Nashua to Lowell. Few if any passenger trains were in those days run in the night and we were accommodated at the famous old Marlboro Hotel in Boston. Here there was no bar, and worship was observed every morning and evening. The iron horse was harnessed early on Tuesday. No checks or guarantees were given for baggage; to insure its safety, we had to see our own in the car and "look after it." We did not go on to Springfield and then northward, as you do now, but stopped off at Wilbraham and took the hypotenuse of the right-angled triangle across the country. We always smile when we recall the station-agent at Wilbraham. He was a small man, excitable, pompous. The advent of the seminary girls was the day of days at that depot. He rose to the situation. It was not gallantry, but business. Napoleon at Marengo never gave the word of command louder or faster. We were soon stowed away in three Concord stage-coaches, each bearing the trade-mark of Abbott and Downing, known then and now the world over. Filled inside and outside, how gently they rocked and swung and swayed!

This first journey ended at the north front door of the seminary. Miss Lyon was the first to meet us. Her beautiful countenance,—for we insist her countenance was beautiful, notwithstanding the oil painting in the seminary hall,—her beautiful countenance glowed with interest and love. The grasp of her hand was hearty, her whole manner cordial and sincere. There was nothing professional or patronizing about her. All the while, we had an inward consciousness that she took our gauge and knew that we would better be assigned to the circle for picking over rice than to the baking circle. We gave her our name. The smile of welcome on her face deepened as she said, "Oh yes, Miss W. from B." We verily believe, that, as the Good Shepherd "calleth his own sheep by name," so Miss Lyon knew and called each one of us by name long before she looked upon us,—yea, more, that she had borne each one of us by name to the mercy-seat.

Our year began in October. The nights and mornings were cool. Each room was warmed by a cheery, little, open Franklin stove. A pair of bellows, to evoke and fan the latent flame, was a necessary article of furniture. Wood was used for heating purposes all over the building. Less than ten years before and bits of anthracite from Pennsylvania lay as curiosities on mantel boards and were passed from neighbor to neighbor in New England with the remark, "They say that this is to be the coming fuel!" The north wing was then an inclosed wood-shed, its stories answering to those of the main building and each bin numbered according to the rooms. The wood was neatly prepared by Mr. Hyde, the man of all work. We never called him by his first name, "Cornelius," or any other prefix. America was not as young then as now. We always said "Mr. Hyde." This Mr. Hyde was not garrulous, but was patient, kind, capable. His skillful hands took the kinks out of refractory locks, blinds, pumps, and what not. As the first servant of Mt. Holyoke Seminary, he rounded out his destiny more symmetrically and honorably than many a monarch.

Friction matches we had, but they were expensive. We learned how to save them by burying a live brand with burning coals under a heap of ashes at night. Thus quick work was made of the morning fire.

Everybody then believed that Job was in a state of poetical rhapsody when he said, "The rock poured me out rivers of oil," and Isaiah when he wrote, "I will utterly divide the tongue of the Egyptian sea." Kerosene was not dreamed of in the one case, or the Suez Canal in the other. Now we see the prophecies were literal. But the rock was not uncapped for us. Hardy sailors from New Bedford went down into the very jaws of death in the Pacific ocean and Arctic seas to fill our lamps. A double tube allowed the passage of two small wicks. These were uncovered. There were no chimneys to crack or to clean. You might smile should we now introduce a tableau showing you how we often lighted our lamps by the aid of a pair of tongs, a coal of fire, and the human breath.

The powers ruling then at Washington were indicated by a log-cabin beautifully wrought in the corner of a black silk apron, worn by a young lady of æsthetic taste. It stood for "Tippecanoe and Tyler too." Take notice, "the barrel of cider," the accompaniment of the log-cabin in the political procession, had no place on the apron. No Holyoke girl, even before the days of the Woman's Christian Temperance Union, would have tolerated such an emblem. We have said that William Henry Harrison was president, but cotton was king. Robert Peel and the Corn Laws did not disturb us, but certain ominous sounds were ever and anon heard in the air. Some called to mind a heathen proverb and declared they were the harsh noises made by the "mills of the gods, grinding slow but exceeding fine." Others thought them the low mutterings of thunder portending a coming storm,—"blood and fire and vapor of smoke." Would you believe it, these sounds were audible now and then even here? Go into a large, airy apartment, second story, main building, east side, used temporarily as a lodging-room for third room-mates, and listen. It is a still night in summer. The lights are out, but the tardy bell has not struck. Some one speaks the word "slavery." Hear the rumbling,—see the flash! Nos. 1 and 2 are instantly arrayed in sentiment against one occupant of No. 3.

Nos. 1 and 2: "I tell you, girls, there's nothing right about slavery! It's all wrong, horribly wrong."

No. 3: "The Bible approves of slavery. Didn't the Israelites hold slaves?"

Nos. 1 and 2: "That's altogether a different thing. Many of them were freed the seventh year, and all the fiftieth."

No. 3: "Well, didn't Paul say, 'Servants, obey in all things your masters'? and servants means slaves. And Paul sent Onesimus, the fugitive slave, back to Philemon, his master."

Nos. 1 and 2: "We looked that out once in Barnes' Notes, and Mr. Barnes says that 'servants' were not all slaves,—and as for Onesimus, Paul didn't send him back as a slave but as a brother beloved."

No. 3 answers with an *argumentum ad hominem:* "If all your father's property were in slaves, would you wish him to free them and make you a pauper?"

Nos. 1 and 2 again: "Yes, yes, a thousand times! Who would want money that was the price of blood?"

Just then a teacher appears in the door. All subside. And here we may say that the pupils of this school have ever been patriotic. Patriotism is not religion, but it is a poor religion that does not include patriotism. At a very early day, Governor Slade, a distinguished philanthropist, went through the Eastern States, taking with him companies of pious and educated ladies to teach in the West. Not a few South Hadley girls enlisted in this first "New West Commission." They married and their sons took up the sword for God and freedom. In Wisconsin, many of these were grouped in one company. Although they were young, some of them very young, so proverbial was their bravery, that where the battle raged the fiercest and picked men and true were needed, the officers would call out, "Slade's boys, come on!"

Let us go back to the opening school and pay the first installment on our bill for board and tuition to Deacon Andrew W. Porter, the first treasurer. The amount was thirty dollars, sixty dollars being the price for one school-year of forty-two weeks! Deacon Porter would have ranked along side Adoniram and Hilkiah, who "took the tribute money" and "summed the silver." We prefer to liken him to Andrew, the first disciple called by our Lord, whose namesake he was. With a business sagacity which made wholesale houses in New York, dealing annually in their millions, covet him as their cashier, and the American Board at Boston desire his services in the same line, he gave himself to the financial interests of this institution with a devotion hardly surpassed by Miss Lyon herself. When the addition was made to our first building, Deacon Porter gave his entire time to the work. After the death of their fourth, their last child, Elizabeth, aged fourteen, there was a renewed consecration of Deacon and Mrs. Porter to this school. With a tremulous voice, Mrs. Porter told us one morning at devotions, that the seminary was henceforth to be their child,—its daughters, their daughters. Some solid silver spoons marked on one side "Mt. Hol. Sem.," on the other, "Elizabeth Porter," found their way at this time to our table.

The first devotional exercise in the seminary hall comes vividly before us. Miss Lyon read and expounded part of the second chapter of Hosea; her theme, an invitation to backsliders to return to God. The melting, especially the searching, influences of the Spirit seemed to descend upon the school from the first gathering. The revival continued through the entire year. Many a hope built alone on resolutions and past experience was thrown away and left forever in the little closet where the "half-hour" had been spent, and, instead, the heart took up the English peasant's couplet,—

"I'm a poor sinner and nothing at all,
But Jesus Christ is my all and in all."

The hymns selected by Miss Lyon were most helpful. She knew a good hymn and could read it well. Ray Palmer and Horatius Bonar had not then struck the lyre, but Rev. Asahel Nettleton, a name the church will never let die, had collected gems from Isaac Watts, Mrs. Steele, Montgomery, and others. This Nettleton's "Village Hymns" was the first hymn book used here. Miss Lyon loved the hymns composed by her personal friends,—one by Mrs. Brown of Monson, "I love to steal awhile away," and, "Say, sinner, hath a voice within," by Mrs. Lavius Hyde. When tired, sick, and overborne with the load she was carrying, it seemed to rest her to give out the hymn,—

"As when the weary traveler gains
The height of some o'erlooking hill,
His heart revives, if 'cross the plains
He eyes his home, though distant still."

Miss Lyon could not sing. This she regretted, but every scholar had to be in one class or another in vocal music. For secular music we used the "Odeon." Some of our new pieces were, "They are gone, all gone from the mountain home," " 'Tis the last rose of summer," and, "Oft in the stilly night." For sacred music, Lowell Mason's "Boston Academy" was the book. Hebron, Boylston, and Ortonville were already beginning to displace Windham, Wells, and St. Martins. We are sure we voice the feeling of a majority here, when we say that the sacred songs at Holyoke have been the sweetest ever remembered on earth. As Christ was made known in the breaking of the bread, so has he been made known here in "holy hymn and psalm" at the morning hour and as the glow of sunset streamed through that green lattice after the evening meal.

Came at length the first Sabbath. We worshiped in the "old white meeting-house." There were three or four tiers of seats in either gallery, rising at an angle of forty-five degrees. The girls occupied the east side, boys and young men, the left. Every sitting was filled. The ventilation was often horrible. But more merciful to us than the sexton were the loosened and multitudinous windows with their "seven by nine" panes of glass, threatening, rattling, and shivering in the wind. With all these drawbacks, the preaching of the Word was "in demonstration of the Spirit and with power." If Deacon Porter, the first treasurer, was a blessing to this institution, so was Rev. Joseph D. Condit, its first pastor. Like Richard Baxter, one foot was ever in the grave. Tall, very tall, slight, ethereal in appearance, he was biblical, clear, impressive in argument and appeal. His preaching seemed always responsive to the spiritual needs of the seminary. He it was who said to Miss Lyon: "I do not have to be informed when the Holy Spirit is with you over there, or when the Sacred Visitant is pluming his wings for flight. The demeanor of the young ladies as they walk to and from church is an unfailing index. It was a glad day for the town and for us, when the new church was dedicated. Mr. Condit had a double text,—"If thy presence go not with me, carry us not up hence." "And He said, My presence shall go with thee, and I will give thee rest. The white-haired "scholars" will seek out Mr. Condit's grave this week as well as Miss Lyon's.

As we are upon "Our First Things," should we be asked to give the sayings of Miss Lyon that come first to our mind after a lapse of forty-five years, these would be among them:—

"Don't allow indulgence in anything sinful or doubtful to come as a wall or even as a mist between you and your Saviour. Does 'this clearing of yourselves' necessitate the mortification of pride, does it necessitate a humble confession to the individual as well as to God, hesitate not for a moment. Go to Christ for strength, then take up the cross, whatever it be. Let your consecration be entire and complete. Keep nothing back."

"Don't try to go as far up as you can to the dividing line between right and wrong. If you are in doubt as to where this line is, give Christ, who died for you, the benefit of the doubt."

"Seek not great things for yourselves, but simply to know your duty and do it. If called by God to the van, shrink not, but in wisdom and humility lead on for Jesus. At the same time be just as willing to perform the lowliest service for the lowliest, although no one save the Master applaud or even appreciate."

"Souls are lost, be in earnest to save them."

"Rejoice and give thanks when other laborers sow and reap better than you can at your best. From your inmost heart pray for such laborers."

"If you are Christ's, you will probably meet with trials. It is right to pray that trials may not come to you. We are taught to pray, 'Lead us not into temptation,' that is, trial. But 'whom the Lord loveth he chasteneth.' When the trial comes, it will be your trial, something that might not try another, but something that will try you. Receive it as an evidence of adoption. Learn the lesson your dear Father would teach you by it. 'Lean hard,' and the reaping shall be the 'peaceable fruits of righteousness.' The greatest trial is to be left of God to live as we list, to float along as does the worldling, losing opportunities and wasting life."—She believed it was possible for even a real Christian, by negligence and unbelief, to invoke this trial.—"The best preparation for the dying hour is present trust. Trust your Redeemer now and he will help you to trust him then."

TO THE MOTHERS.

BY MRS. FRANCIS C. BLAKE, MANSFIELD VALLEY, PA.

(Winifred P. Ballard, '84.)

Do artless eyes, reflecting heaven's blue,
  Look into yours for all their trust and hope?
Do small white hands, that else would blindly grope
Amid world-darkness, tightly cling to you?
Ah mothers, patient be and strong, and true
  To God's divinest mission. Heaven's pure cope
  And earth's fair forms their mysteries do ope
Before thy little child, a rapture new.
  The lily is no purer now than he,
His dewy freshness from the rose he stole,
  Then let no false world-standards taught by thee
Fall like a blight across his unspoiled soul.
  Pray for high faith and love and purity,
That thou mayst show him heaven's highest goal.

EARLY TEACHERS OF MT. HOLYOKE SEMINARY.*

MRS. BURDETT HART, NEW HAVEN, CT.

(Rebecca W. Fiske, '46.)

OF MARY LYON, who stands by herself, mother of us all, what can one say that has not been said by other loyal daughters over and over again? Possibly, to utter the *name*, tenderly, reverently, is our best tribute,—the name that means to us an imperial mind and heart, a peerless pattern of self-forgetting life that cannot fade with the years; that means a character embodying all that is most essential to Christian womanhood in this age of opportunity. For it is as true to-day as when spoken twenty-five years ago, that, "the instant we come down to the common ground of *self-seeking*, we part company with Mary Lyon." We do not wish to part company with her on earthly highways of usefulness, nor on the heavenly hills where the dear familiar face seems awaiting us. One who belongs here to-day, but is detained, writes: "O to think of the day, when we shall be taught again the way of service, by our glorified Miss Lyon! I can picture her there, for I saw her once, rapt in devotion, the full shining of the sun upon her."

---

*This little paper was not evolved on the principle of "the survival of the fittest," but the survival of *memories* growing mainly out of close associations. The selection includes none outside the first decade of the seminary and none "who remain to this day," although they belong to the true line of "succession." The intent is to freshen the portraits hanging in our halls of memory, though no new feature be added.

R. W. H.

Others of us have seen the same face with the light of heaven upon it, in the sanctum, where, in seclusion, she prepared for the large meeting in the seminary hall. The most sacred memory I cherish of her, save those connected with her last hours, is associated with her Bible and the little table which for one year I was privileged to place just as she wished, before the meeting, that even so slight a care might not disturb her sacred moments. Once she said, "Perhaps, my dear, you will love to remember sometime this little service you have done for me." I love at this "sometime" to recall it, and wish the Bible and little table were here. More than once on those occasions the dear face seemed transfigured, as my friend describes it, looking as I love to think it will when she clasps our hands again (if we prove her true daughters) and leads us to higher service and blessedness than we can conceive now in the midst of these earthly limitations and shortcomings.

Looking back to the first decade of the seminary, the lives of the teachers seem so blended, that it were almost as easy to withdraw one face from a composite photograph as to hold one of these grand lives up to view apart from the others.

MISS WHITMAN and MISS MOORE are linked in our thoughts no less than in office as associate principals,—two figures inspiring respect and standing with dignity between the seminary and the public. With their rare common sense and uncommon judgment, Miss Lyon must have found them good to lean upon, as Moses found certain strong arms in his day. And did not Misses Moore and Whitman, in a sense, help to sustain the law of the school, while some of a different type in the sisterhood more fully dispensed the gospel of its love?

Miss Whitman could, on occasion, inspire awe in a wayward girl whom love in milder form had not won to duty. It was whispered among such that her reserve was born of an early romance with a somber side, and that the premature crown of gray had the same origin. But if one failed, while a pupil, to find the warm side of her heart, it was there all the same. I know one who carried her first-born to her *alma mater* when Miss Whitman was principal, and learned what a motherly welcome she had for the grandchildren of the seminary; that mother ever after called Miss Whitman affectionate, mellow-hearted. When she became Mrs. Eddy, and went to preside over the good Deacon's home in Fall River, her nature blossomed out visibly on the domestic side, and there she renewed her youth. Alive to every good cause, while life lasted, she went to her reward twelve years ago.

Miss Abigail Moore seemed an embodiment of strength and serenity. So it was fitting that she should talk to the school on the evils of undue excitement, physical or mental. Her calm manner was a quietus; her face in repose was peace itself. After eight years of usefulness here, she married Rev. Mr. Burgess in 1846, and joined the Marathi mission, spending in India the remaining seven years of her life. For such a nature as hers, the transition from the sweet seminary life to the scenes of heathendom at Bombay must have been shocking in the extreme.

ALUMNÆ MEETING. 59

One who welcomed her there forty years ago says: "She was one of the true, faithful, and judicious women, and her loss to the mission was deeply felt. Very suddenly she was called to leave three motherless daughters, one orphaned at birth. In her last moments she was heard to say, "I think I hear the music of the spheres." She was buried on the Mahabulishur Hills in 1853. Years later a beloved missionary daughter, bearing her name, was laid beside her, the husband and a friend walking eleven miles up the steep mountain side, in order that mother and child might sleep together till the resurrection morning.

MARTHA R. CHAPIN's name follows here, who laid down her seminary work in the same year with Mrs. Burgess, to join the same mission, as the wife of Rev. Allen Hazen. Was not the seminary a little partial to India that year, in giving her two so choice spirits from the corps of teachers, when Ceylon had claimed Susan Reed Howland, and the Madura mission Nancy Foote Webb, not long before? Martha Chapin must have had four sections between '42 and '46, and favored girls were they who had such a section teacher. What a winsome, sunny face she wore, not on occasions, as when Mr. Hazen came a wooing, but uniformly! To see her was to love her; to know her was to love her better; to know her intimately was to be in love thenceforth with the hidden worth of the heart half concealed by her native modesty. Her first term of service in India covered twelve years. She might then have been graduated from the missionary work with high honors, but in '64 she returned and gave eight years more to the loved work. In 1872 she took final leave of India, but was willing still to make sacrifices for that dark land, and thither she sent her heart three years later, in the person of a beloved daughter. Gradually declining, cheerfully submitting, ardently loving her own, and her Saviour, and all those for whom he died, she rested from earthly labors in 1884.

LUCY M. CURTIS of fragrant memory was enrolled as teacher in the seminary from '44 to '49. Her refined, lady-like bearing was as unobtrusive as it was winning. How soft her voice, how light her footstep through the halls! Her words distilled gently like the dew, yet her heart-beats were strong for those she loved,—and whom did she not love? From the standpoint of a room-companion, we can testify to the rare combination of qualities that made her a true woman, whom all must love. The sundering of tenderest ties had changed life's outlook for her; and at the same time came an attack of disease which of itself predicted its return, and made her watchful for the hour which she knew not. Rarely is a person in such ready expectancy for the call homeward as she was for seven years. Yet none suspected that she loved life less for her slight hold upon it. The cheery smile and hearty interest in all about her were perpetual. It was always spring-time in her heart, and this gave a steady life current, whose peaceful outflow nothing ruffled, not even the midnight call of the coming Bridegroom. A few weeks before, she had tenderly ministered to the last needs of her dear Miss Lyon, and she now gladly accepted the tokens that she was soon to join her. With words of peace and victory on her lips, she lingered with home friends a few days, and then joyfully followed Mary Lyon through the gates into the City.

Two of the teachers were specially linked with our class of '46— LUCY T. LYON and FIDELIA FISKE. To Miss Fiske, then three years in Persia, we gave our very best,—Mary Susan Rice,—to be her faithful assistant in Oroomiah Seminary. "Miss Lucy" taught our class Mental Philosophy, clarified our minds over the abstruse things of Butler, and, lending us the wings of her fine imagination, helped us to soar with Milton. The two may be spoken of jointly in some aspects, while they were quite unlike in others. Both were born in Franklin county, we are proud to say; Miss Lucy in the same Buckland honored as the birthplace of Mary Lyon, by whom both were dearly loved. Both were so true to all truth that undue praise of them would be unseemly. They were both endowed generously with intellect, with strong, forceful willpower, and with warm affectional natures. They could do their own thinking and loving. Their sympathies were world wide. Both had that best heritage—a godly ancestry, and each professed the faith in which she was reared at about fourteen years of age. Neither became our heroine from the enchantment of the distant Orient, but the closer we came to the inner personality of each, the more cause we found to enshrine her in our hearts. To each of them this seminary was the most endeared spot on earth, and each, after laying down foreign missionary work, returned here as naturally as the dove to the ark. Both had fellowship with Christ in extremity of suffering at the last, and in perfect submission to the Father's will.

Lucy T. Lyon was one of ten children, and so her nature, touched on all sides, was rounded and enriched in her childhood's home. She longed for the higher education with all her intense spirit, and bravely overcame all obstacles, till she attained this ideal seminary life, and after two years graduated in 1840. She taught in the seminary with increasing ability from 1841 to 1846. Many of us remember her uplifting prayers, and the ring of confidence she gave to Scripture readings, notably that passage of Isaiah, "*Doubtless* thou art our Father, though Abraham be ignorant of us and Israel acknowledge us not: thou, O Lord, art our Father, *our Redeemer*." Who would have thought she had dwelt much in "Doubting Castle" until she came within the clear Christian atmosphere of these consecrated walls, here to find the "Chamber of Peace" if not the "Delectable Mountains"?

Her desire for missionary work abroad, if not born here, received stimulus and growth from the biblical teachings of Miss Lyon, and from other quickening influences. We know that some of her roommates did not disguise their desire in that direction. Of these were Fidelia Fiske; and the "beloved Persis," who kept the heathen in mind by playfully naming herself our "heathen sister"; also Susan Reed, surnamed Howland, now mother of missionaries; and her dear cousin, Mrs. Burgess, to whom her last letter was addressed. In the same year these two nieces, so helpful, were given up by Miss Lyon to India and China. "Miss Lucy" became Mrs. Edward C. Lord and with her husband sailed for China, January, 1847. After five years of earnest endeavor, and failure of. health, she found it harder to turn away from Ningpo than it had been to leave her native land.

In going from Boston to her home friends by short stages, she rested for a few days in my home. As she was borne within like an infant, it was difficult at once to recognize "Miss Lucy" there, but rest soon brought back the old vivacity, and her identity was unmistakable. She was sanguine at times in the hope of return to China, but greatly chastened in spirit, by what she had endured. How proudly her letters had told of "Master Edward, the young nobleman, descended from Lords and Lyons;" but now, with pathos in her submission, she talked of her two angel children waiting on high to greet their mother. After some months with her friends in western New York her native resolution asserted itself, and she came to the seminary for her last visit in the summer of 1852. On May 5, 1853, she went peacefully from her home in Fredonia to the home of the blessed. The "rod" and the "staff" they comforted her, in the "valley."

Of Fidelia Fiske how can one be trusted to speak, fairly or briefly, who was a near neighbor for years and close friend for a lifetime? Her life story has been told by an able pen. Appended to the record of Dr. Fiske are manifold tributes of just and loving appreciation. Language could not delineate more perfectly the character of Miss Fiske than her associate for eleven years has done in that appendix. Fifteen years of unbroken service in Persia have furnished the material, largely, for two volumes of exceptional and thrilling interest. There can be few present who are not familiar with these, and with Miss Fiske's "Recollections of Mary Lyon," in which the personality of the author is unavoidably revealed. There is no need to go over to-day the well-trodden ground of her missionary work in Persia. It may be better that we linger for a little on the Shelburne hills, and mainly within the walls of the ancestral home, where three generations were domiciled. Fidelia's grandfather often peopled his room with those also of a previous generation, whom she had not seen. Here she came to revere the great-grandmother—great, in two senses, especially great in prayer, so that Fidelia wished her name, Dorcas Tyler, had been given to herself. But Fidelia the Faithful was well-named, and was a lineal child of the praying Dorcas. This same room was the scene of the birth, marriage, and death of her own father. Here the patriarch grandfather blessed his son Pliny as he went forth on his pioneer mission, when the niece Fidelia was three years old. Here were read her uncle Pliny's letters from Jerusalem, till the little girl naturally played missionary, and ran to her mother one day to tell her she had "been to Jerusalem in the wheelbarrow." And so when a mere child she longed to be a Christian that she might be a missionary. Here the quick scholar and thoughtful child prepared her school-day lessons, and reveled in reading that which few children relish. When six years old she would climb to the top of the primitive "drawers" for the *Missionary Herald*, that she might read it aloud to her mother; and with no effort at mental climbing enjoyed reading, twice through, "Dwight's Theology," at eight. Her early teaching in the common schools did not omit the department of theology. She lived the Bible, and taught it prominently to all her pupils. She loved to recall in her latest days one dear boy of nine years who studied with her the "minor prophets" after school hours, and whose course she followed into the ministry and to a soldier's grave. She taught with such success as her tact and lovingness made sure, for six years before she saw Mt. Holyoke Seminary, the lowly house by the lofty elm being her home on Sundays and in vacations.

Here, in the east room, in 1840, after a year at the seminary, she was brought low by illness, and went even down into the "valley of the shadow," where she was sure her Saviour met her, spoke to her, and assured her of his love. Reluctantly she came back to a life more than ever given to Christ, and never afterward could she think of a dying Christian as being at all alone. While slowly recovering, the dear father and a sister were fatally stricken with the same disease; and in her grief then she learned to "lean hard" upon infinite love, long before the Nestorian woman suggested the same lesson. On the night after the house had been left so desolate by the second visit of the death angel there occurred in the family room an object lesson never to be forgotten,—the convalescing Fidelia, in her favorite position, upon the floor at her mother's feet, calmly striving to console the broken heart in its double bereavement. Her plaintive words will ever live in my heart.

To this same home came Miss Lyon with Fidelia by an open sleigh-ride of thirty miles, in February, 1843, in peril of cold, and in peril of snowdrifts in which they were overturned more than once, arriving late on Saturday night. "The King's business" required haste; the question of going to Persia must be referred again to the widowed mother, who had before withheld her consent. There was no retiring bell there that night, and little sleep. Before the Sabbath had passed, the word had been spoken,—" Go, my child, go." During the week that followed how busy were our hands in that same west room where such heart-work had been done on Sunday. As by magic there and at the seminary the outfit was prepared in very few days, yet in these and later boxes many articles of taste as well as of vesture went to missionary ground; for our Fidelia never affected indifference to dress, but believed that the influence of a missionary was enhanced by what is becoming and attractive.

And now, passing over her work for the Nestorians, with its marvelous results, as well as her added years of high service at the seminary between '58 and '64, with their spiritual fruitage, we find her in Shelburne again, on a bright summer day in '64, five weeks before she fell asleep. She had now one strong desire left,—to live long enough to complete the book she had undertaken—" The Recollections "—and insisted upon reading at intervals during the day some chapters of manuscript, craving helpful suggestions. But soon she sweetly passed the incomplete volume to other hands. This was the last surrender of her own choice to the divine will. She had once written: "How much we might enjoy in this life if God's will were always ours." Now she had reached that ideal of the Christian. Suffering silently, and expecting to suffer more intensely, she could say with humble, impressive confidence, "I can look beyond." On the morning of July 26, a ministerial friend was granted admission to her room. Her response to his greeting was, "Will you pray?" These words were her last, a call to prayer. Before the petitions ended she had answered the call to praise.

We began our sketch with one, and close with another, who vainly longed through life to sing the songs of the earthly Zion. We love to think that no purer, sweeter notes mingle in the "new song" of the heavenly Zion than those of Mary Lyon and Fidelia Fiske.

Mrs. Hart's paper was followed by the trio, "O memory."

EARLY TRUSTEES.

It was hoped till a very late day that a paper on the trustees would be presented by the surviving member of the class of '38. When this hope failed, the following facts were collated by Mrs. Sarah Looke Stow, '59.

By the seminary charter, granted February, 1836, "Hon. William Bowdoin of South Hadley Falls, Rev. John Todd of Northampton, Rev. Joseph D. Condit of South Hadley, Hon. David Choate of Essex, and Hon. Samuel Williston of Easthampton, their associates and successors," were constituted the board of trustees. These five met March 5, and added to their number Rev. William Tyler of South Hadley Falls, and Rev. Roswell Hawks of Cummington. Joseph Avery of Conway was elected April 13, and Andrew W. Porter of Monson, April 19.

Mr. Todd and Mr. Williston having resigned the same year, their places were filled October 3 by the election of President Heman Humphrey and Professor Edward Hitchcock of Amherst College. April 3, 1837, Daniel Safford of Boston was added to the board. Mr. Williston was re-elected in 1839 and remained in office till 1862. Mr. Tyler and Mr. Bowdoin each served twenty years and resigned in 1856.

Dr. HUMPHREY's connection with the board continued from 1836 to 1846, ending the year after his resignation of the presidency at Amherst. He returned in 1847 to deliver the anniversary address, and in 1849 to preach the sermon at Miss Lyon's funeral.

Mr. CHOATE was one of Miss Lyon's Ipswich friends, of whom it is said "she seldom spoke without a moistened eye." Though at first desirous to have the seminary located in the eastern part of the state, when that was found impracticable he united in the effort to bring it into the Connecticut valley, and is said to be one of the two persons who first selected the site on which the main building stands; the other was Mr. Hawks. That he continued to watch the progress of the seminary with unabated interest after his resignation in 1843, appears from his letter published in the memorial of the twenty-fifth anniversary.

REV. JOSEPH D. CONDIT become pastor of the church in South Hadley, July 8, 1835, six months after that place was fixed upon for the location of the seminary. Miss Lyon found in him a warm friend who sympathized in all her plans; and while attending to the finishing and furnishing of the seminary building she was received into his family as a sister.

Mr. Condit delivered the address at the dedication of the new seminary May 3, 1838, and presented their diplomas to the first graduating class.

September 10, 1847, Miss Lyon wrote: "Our dear Mr. Condit is very near his home. The king of terrors is approaching with gentle step as if loth to take his prey. Here I am alone in this great building; no one near to interrupt my grief. I love this solitude, for tears and prayers in his behalf. The years of our acquaintance pass in rapid review. As I dwell on him as a friend, a Christian, a counselor, a pastor,—sadness spreads over my soul. And yet it is not all sorrow. Heaven seems to be opening her gates to receive another servant of Christ." He died September 19th.

REV. ROSWELL HAWKS had for years been studying how to secure greater educational advantages for young women. In May, 1834, he said to Dr. Packard, in Boston, "I want to confer with you in regard to a plan for the education of the daughters of our land." Dr. Packard replied, "If you have that in view you should see Miss Lyon of Ipswich, who is here for the same purpose." She was not unknown to him, for he had sent a daughter to her school in Buckland.

They met; Mr. Hawks, entering heartily into Miss Lyon's project, declared himself ready to do anything in his power to forward it, and from that day onward, no person was a more patient listener to her plans or a more sincere co-worker in their execution. She came to have such confidence in his judgment that she would undertake no important measure without first consulting him, and neither would adopt a course the other did not favor.

When called to give up his pastorate in Cummington to become sole agent for collecting funds for the establishment of the future seminary, his people were unwilling to relinquish him; he was assured that he had mistaken his duty; the scheme of a seminary for women was ridiculed and he was thought by some to be of unsound mind. But his whole heart was enlisted and he entered without delay upon the task of raising funds for the project called chimerical by some and by some even wicked. How his faith triumphed is attested by the very walls of the seminary; but the fatigue, cold, and hunger he endured in his journeyings, that the funds of the seminary should not be lessened for his needs, was then known only to God and himself; in after years it became known to his family.

Mr. Hawks did a similar work for Lake Erie Seminary in Painesville, Ohio, but his love for the first child of his toils and prayers was strong to the end. In his last visit to the seminary, a few months before his death, it was beautiful to see that although his days of active labor were over, his devotion to Christ in all its fullness still remained. An attack of paralysis closed his long life of eighty-two years, April 10, 1870. A long procession followed his remains to the grave. The young ladies gathered around it and sang "Rest for the toiling hand," and then the venerable form was laid to rest, as he requested, within sight of the seminary walls and within sound of its bells.

Mr. Hawks was president of the board of trustees from 1838 to 1858; his trusteeship extended from 1836 till the time of his death, a period of thirty-four years.

DEA. JOSEPH AVERY.—When Miss Lyon was soliciting funds for the seminary, in Conway, she was the guest of Deacon Joseph Avery, of whom she wrote January 11, 1836: "During the past twenty years he has probably given more to benevolent objects in proportion to his property and family than any other man in New England. I was delighted with the godly simplicity, well balanced views, and systematic benevolence of the family."

For several years this good man gave the seminary substantial aid from his rock-bound farm. Like Miss Lyon, he could not bear to see a cent of the sacred funds of the seminary go for naught. At one time when an architect's plan had been purchased which did not prove available, he paid the bill in addition to his large subscription. This kind deed, at a time when her own purse was poorly able to bear another draft, Miss Lyon never forgot. When he could give no more in money toward the first building, he came to South Hadley and gave the labor of his hands day after day. Deacon Avery was a progressive man. After the addition to the building in 1842, when the trustees with some anxiety faced the question whether the new seminary hall should be carpeted, he was one of the first to approve the outlay, saying, "The times demand it. The education of the world is being carried on here." His term of office continued from 1836 until his death in 1855.

COL. AUSTIN RICE of Conway, elected in 1858, was one of the early friends of education for woman. With a few others he met Miss Lyon at Dr. Hitchcock's in Amherst to listen to her plans and give advice, when most men regarded them as a quixotic dream. From that day to the end of his life in 1880 he was an unwavering friend of the seminary. Nearly eighty-six when he died, his attendance at trustee meetings for twenty-two years had been almost without interruption.

REV. EDWARD HITCHCOCK was one of the fathers and founders of the seminary. He and Mrs. Hitchcock had been friends of Miss Lyon from her girlhood; the prominence of natural science in the seminary course may be traced to the enthusiasm she caught from Dr. Hitchcock when in his family in Conway. In their home in Amherst she spent the winter after leaving Ipswich, in 1834. There they invited a joint committee from Essex county and the Connecticut valley to meet her and examine her plans. Thence Dr. Hitchcock went with her at one time to Worcester, and at another to Boston, when important questions about the future seminary were to be discussed and decided. To the seminary classes he lectured in natural sciences, and he was probably the first donor to the cabinet of minerals, and also to the ichnological cabinet. In his wisdom Miss Lyon always confided, saying in every emergency, "I must consult my good friend Dr. Hitchcock."

The intimacy of his acquaintance with her made it fitting that he should edit the story of her life. His last visit to the seminary was at its twenty-fifth anniversary, and his closing words to the school were those so often on his lips, "The everlasting foundations are sure." He died in 1864, having been trustee twenty-eight years.

ANDREW W. PORTER.—After the seminary charter was obtained and a location fixed upon, some one was needed to superintend the work of building. Dea. A. W. Porter was mentioned, and Mr. Hawks and Mr. Tyler, in company with Miss Lyon, were appointed to lay the matter before him. On arriving at his home in Monson on Saturday, they learned that Mr. Porter was in Boston and would not return until evening. Miss Lyon remained over the Sabbath. She retired to her room before Mr. Porter arrived and not a word was said about the seminary till Monday. Ten or twelve years later she told Mrs. Porter that those were nights of prayer. "And the Lord," said she, "not only answered my prayer by inclining your husband to engage in the work, but gave me yourself and Mr. Porter as personal friends, and your house as my home."

Mr. Porter was soon as active in the enterprise as if it were his own; he was not only on the first building-committee but continued to act in that capacity whenever building was to be done during his forty years of devoted service for the seminary. While the first building was in progress he spent several days each week at South Hadley; from March to November, nearly every Monday he drove there, twenty-one miles, returning home Saturday. During all this time he left his own extensive business in other hands, provided his own conveyance, entertained himself and horse, and made no charge whatever. Through life every interest of the seminary continued to be the object of his conscientious care and constant prayers. A Holyoke pupil writes, "Miss Lyon never forgot to tell us of Deacon Porter's absence on her first visit, and of her two days of seeking to be willing to give up securing his aid, before she could even talk with him; then she would add, 'And now don't you think God has given us in Deacon Porter the very best man his storehouse could furnish?'"

Deacon Porter was at the seminary for the last time at the dedication of the Lyman Williston Hall. Though he then seemed as well as usual, and in full sympathy with the gladness of the occasion, it became evident during the winter that a disease of the heart, from which he had long suffered, was advancing to a fatal termination. As he lay in his reclining chair with closed eyes, apparently beyond intercourse with earth, those about him observed that he was moving his finger as if writing. They placed a pencil in his hand, and paper beneath it;

the faltering hand, which the eye could no longer guide, traced the words, "Messages of love to all seminary daughters." Repeating the effort, as if doubtful whether he had succeeded, he wrote, "Love to all pupils of seminary." That penciled message is treasured among the most sacred mementos which the seminary possesses of its departed friends. Two days after completing his eighty-second year, on Sabbath morning, March 4, 1877, he fell asleep.

His one anxiety in his later years had been to see others come forward to undertake the work that he must lay down. His desire had been granted; in a letter two years before his death, he had spoken of the comfort it gave him to have "two such men as Mr. Williston and Mr. Sawyer, so competent and so willing, to afford us their aid, at a time when they are so much needed. I have been thankful every time I have had the seminary on my mind lately that we have these new helpers to lean upon."

But Mr. Sawyer's brief term of six years was ended in 1879 by his lamented death.

MR. A. L. WILLISTON, a trustee since 1867, as treasurer of the board and chairman of the executive committee, took up the self-sacrificing work that Deacon Porter laid down and continues to carry it on with the same fidelity. The observatory, the hall that bears his name, and many of the arrangements of the jubilee occasion testify no less to his large beneficence than to his foresight and his patient care for unforgotten details.

DANIEL SAFFORD.—More than once in 1836 Daniel Safford of Boston had been mentioned to Miss Lyon as just the man to help forward her enterprise. Unknown to her, Providence had been preparing the way. Mrs. Safford had read Dr. Hitchcock's newspaper articles about the "Pangynaskian Seminary" and had told the story to her husband. Miss Lyon, having ventured to write him about her project, was invited to his house. "Between the ringing of the door-bell and the response," she used to say years after, "I tried to roll all my care upon the Lord, and be willing to receive not one encouraging word, if so my God would be most honored." As she unfolded her plans, watching intently every expression of her hearers, she saw that they listened with eager interest, but had then no knowledge of the way the Lord had prepared them for her visit. From that day Deacon Safford's interest in the seminary increased until it became his favorite work, occupying his thoughts as well as receiving his money, and filling scarcely a smaller place in his affections than in Miss Lyon's. "What I have given to Mt. Holyoke Seminary," said he, "I consider the best investment I have ever made; there is no depreciation in the stock; it yields the largest dividends." But the time, influence, and sympathy which he and his wife gave to it were worth more than their thousands of silver and gold. His last labors for the seminary were in connection with the finishing of the old library room. His gifts to the first building fund amounted to $4,000, and at the time of his death, in 1856, he was the largest donor to the seminary.

"There was always joy in the house," wrote a teacher, "when it was announced that Deacon Safford had come. With a quick sympathy and delicate playfulness he inquired into the affairs of the house,—wood, water, changes in the building, the wherewith by which the multitude should be fed, domestic and pecuniary affairs generally. We brought our wants and perplexities and spread them out freely before him. But sweeter counsel did we take together on the spiritual welfare of our household. It was this which most deeply interested him, and the simple, earnest expressions of his own dependence on the quickening Spirit often brought us low with him before God.

"From its beginning he assumed the task of making for the seminary its large and frequent purchases of groceries and a variety of other articles. He planned and directed the introduction of water into different parts of the building, and repeatedly spent weeks in superintending building or other improvements. Even in his brief visits, he was busy looking about the house and grounds to see what was wanting. Still he never seemed to think that he did any great things, and it was quite embarrassing to try to thank him for his kindnesses. Little did we think when he promised to bring his minister the next time he came that when Dr. Kirk should come it would be alone, to speak in commemoration of our departed friend."

The name of REV. EDWARD N. KIRK, D.D., though he was not one of the earliest trustees, should not be omitted from this list. His election in 1856 filled the place made vacant by the death of Deacon Safford. Dr. Kirk followed Mr. Hawks as president in 1858 and held that office till his death in 1874, and was himself succeeded by the present honored incumbent, Rev. Wm. S. Tyler, D.D., who has been a member of the board for twenty-five years, and who, we hope, will remain its president as long as he lives.

Dr. Kirk met Miss Lyon first at the house of Deacon Safford when Miss Fiske was leaving for Persia. His first visit to the seminary was in 1844, when he made the anniversary address. He came next in 1855, and after that time as often as once a year, frequently choosing the day of prayer for colleges. Teachers and students welcomed him as a friend and counselor, and hundreds of souls will forever bless God for his faithful words. Especially fruitful were his labors here in February, 1864. After his sight failed and he had given up all other public efforts, he still enjoyed spending a few weeks at a time with us, and exerting the last of his failing strength in our behalf. He sought for the seminary the greatest usefulness, and accordingly in the words of Dr. Tyler: "He always insisted on the necessity of keeping the seminary ever in the foremost rank of schools and colleges for the sex; as in Christian character and life, so in the standard of scientific attainment, literary culture, and all high and true womanhood. . . . .
While he contended earnestly for the faith and spirit of the founders, and insisted on keeping the seminary true to the principles on which, and the purposes for which, it was established, he was never afraid of innovations which were in the line of real progress. Indeed, he often

ALUMNÆ MEETING.

remarked that the seminary was one great innovation, and Mary Lyon herself the greatest of innovators."

To catch more of his spirit let us listen again to his own words spoken at our reunion twenty-five years ago :—

"This unusual gathering of teachers and alumnæ shows how much this school is beloved of God's children. There cannot be a question that it is already a vast power in our nation, both as a part of the great educational machinery of our country, and as founded on lofty Christian principles. The question that awakens our solicitude is, Will its guardians prove faithful to their trust? It is no common piety that can keep it where its founder left it. A decleusion of piety in the churches would come stealthily up here like the miasma of death. If the churches cease to pray for it, the blessing of God will be proportionally diminished. This seminary is a sacred trust from the Lord to his churches. If the trustees should come to regard it in a merely secular light, their influence will be hurtful rather than beneficial. If the teachers should come down from the high places of prayer, of close walking with God; if worldly ambition and self-seeking should gain possession of their hearts,—it would so far fail of its original design, and the most sacred of trusts be so far betrayed.

"Fellow trustees! we are guardians of an institution dear to many now in heaven ; dear to him that sits upon its throne. Let us to-day take a new view of our trust and watch ourselves lest we impair some element of its strength. Teachers within those walls! you are laboring for Christ and eternity. The instant you come down to the common ground of self-seeking you part company with Mary Lyon and you betray her dear seminary. May her Saviour keep you as he kept her! Daughters of Holyoke! refresh yourselves with the precious memories of the past. It does a generous soul good to revive its sense of obligation. Remember the goodness of God and praise him. Remember the true-hearted ones that so nobly bore the burden and the reproach of this enterprise in its infancy. Bless God for their noble work ; greet each other here once more; and then go forth to carry out even more fully the sacred principles you were taught here."

PROMINENCE GIVEN TO SCIENCE.

Miss L. W. SHATTUCK, '51, Senior Instructor.

In the very beginning of the seminary, science had a prominent place in its course of study. Botany was in both the first and second years of the three years' course. Chemistry, geology, astronomy, natural philosophy, physiology, and philosophy of natural history had each its appointed place,—seven sciences in a course of twenty-three studies. Names have changed since then and work has broadened; botany and zoology have stretched out into the deeper researches of biology. In chemistry, in the early years, Miss Lyon was the enthusiastic teacher and experimenter. That she was a successful one, several now present can testify.

In geology she listened eagerly to the testimony of the rocks, and joined a party led by President Hitchcock of Amherst on a tour of investigation. At that very time many of his ministerial brethren were branding him as a heretic for his views of the six days of creation. Miss Lyon had none of the spirit of the Brahmin who pulverized the microscope because it showed him animal life in his food. She stood calmly by while the opening leaves of the earth's rocky crust revealed ages between the beginning and the first living thing. I have yet to learn that, because of these studies, any of our students have become less reverent toward the Bible or less confident of the divine love and care. Our non-resident professors give us credit for doing good work in science. One of them recently suggested that in future, as a college, we give a special scientific direction to our pursuits, "For," said he, "there is an earnest spirit of study here favorable to scientific research, and science does not tolerate any half way work."

Since, therefore, the instruction of the seminary has had a scientific trend from the first without tendency to convert us into agnostics or infidels, since this is a scientific age and we are bound to keep abreast of the times, since every college has its own particular individuality, let us press onward in these lines till we obtain full recognition among the colleges of New England, claiming the right to confer degrees whenever it can be shown that our pupils have done as much and as good work as other colleges require for the same degrees.

You will pardon a few words of personal reminiscence and grateful acknowledgment. Some of you will remember our long walks together in search of oxalis and orchids, gold-thread and lady's slippers. Some of you have been lost on mountain and plain in the interests of science. Some of you have made us glad by gifts to the botanical garden and the gift of the greenhouse. From many we have had kind letters and kind wishes and multitudes of helpful words and deeds. The lengthening shadows remind some of us that it is almost time to go home and rest. In that glad morning, when the tireless spirit shall be clad in a body as tireless as itself, when our eyes shall see the King in his beauty and we shall behold the land that is very far off, where our Elder Brother shall wrap all who are his own in the vestments of fine linen, pure and white, may we, every one, be found at his right hand.

THE STONE OF SCONE.

MRS. HANNAH HUNT CANDEE, '58, LOWELL.

THE winds that blow across the sea
Bring echoes of the jubilee.

Fair Albion's Queen still holds the throne,
Crowned Queen upon the stone of Scone.

And banners wave and flowers bloom,
  And music fills the air;
"God save the Queen!" "God save the Queen!"
  Resounding everywhere.

Plantagenet and Tudor. How
  The stately march moves on,
Crowned all upon the stone of fate,
  From Scotia's kingdom won.

The sacred stone of destiny,
  The coronation stone,
Where pillowed lay the patriarch's head,
  On rocky height alone.

The stone of vision, for he saw
  A ladder reaching high,
With angels moving up and down,
  And God above the sky.

The stone of consecration, as
  The oil on it was poured;
"This cairn shall be the house of God,
  This God shall be adored."

See clouds of arrows in their flight,
And Bethel's stone is lost in night.

To fierce and warlike Scythian hordes,
  A charm the cromlech brings;
Like winds that murmur through the pines
  "God save the King!" it sings.

On sunny slopes of vine-clad Spain,
  The storied stone may rest,
Till thirty sea birds slowly sail
  To Erin's sheltered nest.

And where, when Tara's halls are mute,
  Shall rest the stone of Scone?
Where the rude monastery crowns
  Iona's island lone.

The dauntless vikings sought the shrines
 Of Ion's peaceful shore;
Macalpine brave the treasured stone
 To rugged Scotland bore.

In great Westminster's royal seat
 Now rests the stone of Scone.
God save the Queen, who sheds the light
 Of truth round England's throne!

Holyoke and Tom stand sentinel
 With clouds around their brow,
They long have kept the castle gate,
 True, faithful warders now.

    Mount Holyoke, Queen this side the sea,
    Her children calls to jubilee.

    Our Queen sits on her emerald throne,
    The rock of prayer her stone of Scone.

    Her corner-stone the rock of prayer,
    Her vision is a palace fair—

    That rests on earth, but reaches high
    Above the blue and arching sky.

Our Queen the royal handmaid is
 Of the great King of kings,
Whose praise, with all his loyal clans,
 Our Queen forever sings.

And like the merchant ships that sail
 To distant climes afar,
Her messengers go forth with bread
 To those that waiting are.

No ruby's flash, nor diamond's ray,
 Adorns her regal crown,
More pure than pearl or chrysolite
 Is wisdom's fair renown.

With strength and honor is she clad,
 Her lips speak love's own law,
In ever widening vistas, opes
 The vision that she saw.

No dream of ruined palaces,
 No palm of victories won,
Its towers in beauty still shall rise,
 In strength shall still grow on.

So, in her mountain-girdled seat,
We bow and kiss her blessed feet,

And pray, Be bright her crystal sheen;
God save our Queen! God save our Queen!

For who the heavenly vision heeds,
Whom the true Stone of Israel leads,

Shall lead in white, her children free,
Home coming for their jubilee.

REMINISCENCES.

MRS. THOMAS CARTER, BOONTON, N. J.
(Hettie M. Dodd, '71.)

AN incident in Mrs. Burnett's story of "Haworth's" suggested itself forcibly, as I watched the throng that poured into the registration tent yesterday. Those of you who have read it will remember "Mr. Briarley," the man of "misforchnit habits" and "patient mendacity." He comes in from the "public" one day, with hesitant hilarity, and his better half, Sararann, discovers that he has joined the strikers. She is in no mood for trifling. She goes to the door and summons all the little Briarleys, of assorted sizes, from the street. They rush into the room, tumbling over each other, helter-skelter, the whole dozen of them, filling the room full to overflowing. Generally they were disposed of in relays, for convenience' sake, and, Mr. Briarley's large capacity for beer keeping him much at the "public," he had seldom seen the whole array. He sits upright, and stares at them. Sararann confronts him like an accusing conscience, saying only, "Them's your hoffspring—them is!" and poor Mr. Briarley, unable to cope with the situation, sinks helplessly into a chair, saying, with an air of meek protestation: "Send 'em out in the air, Sararann;—they seems to have accumylated! *They certainly seems to ha' accumylated!*"

Alma mater might be pardoned a gesture of dismay at the cumulative nature of her offspring, as the never ceasing stage-loads empty themselves at the gates,—but she is neither overwhelmed nor perplexed. Without stopping to take breath, she turns to greet each fresh installment, and the hundred-and-forty-eleventh stage-load is as welcome as the first. We always knew she was equal to any emergency, but then we are proud of it just the same.

We have been living over school-days for weeks past, in anticipation of this event. We have climbed into the attic of memory, and hunted on the top shelves, and are jubilant over the revelation of lost treasures. In spite of the proverbial stupidity of school-girl journals, I improved a permission to look one through the other day, and it proved a veritable mine of happy memories. It was kept in "room 44" during '69 and '71, and the mere mention of familiar names was enough to make the tears come. It opened first at some invectives leveled at the Miscellaneous Circle (that did not appeal to the pathetic, exactly!). Evidently the writer was in a "state of mind." She objected to its being made the purgatory through which superfluous juniors chopped and peeled their way to more aristocratic circles. She resented still more, its being a sort of Botany Bay for irrepressible middlers, who talked more than they chopped,—or, for "old pokes," who couldn't do either! She considered the leadership of the Miscellaneous Circle unequaled as a means of grace, looked at in the light of discipline, and regarded canonization as a mild reward for six weeks' experience. Possibly some of the rest of us remember that it was not the leaders only who got the discipline.

Further on, there is a picture of Miss French as she sat at the desk at morning devotions. To those of us who knew her, no description could do her justice; and those who did not have missed so much that we will not aggravate their loss by dwelling on it. When we call to mind the clear, sweet common-sense of her morning talks at devotions,—the way in which she held a mirror to our unspoken thoughts, and opened up unused avenues of conscience, and encouraged every germ of right effort,—we only wonder that we are not better women than we are!

Then follows a reference to Prof. J. H. Seelye's lecture on "The Sun"—and the much learning of the incipient senior crops out in a sage comparison of his views with Prof. Young's. Nowadays we speak of astronomy with bated breath, having no fixed ideas of anything but the Dipper, and a few shreds of class-lore not included in the text books,—as for instance when a much embarrassed classmate, trying to retrieve herself in a sadly tangled recitation, emerged with the triumphant explanation that the "tail of the Dipper was the handle of the Great Bear!" We mention Prof. Young's name, now, with reverence, and hear with awe of Miss Bardwell's observatory work, and the adjustments of the new telescope—but then, when we were middlers, we could indulge in such comparisons. It *is* uplifting to think that once we knew all about the sun!

The carefully-repressed feeling that "we are the middlers, and wisdom dies with us," underlying some of these pages, is delightfully suggestive of the time when we knew more than we ever shall again. Alas for the evanescence of middlerhood!

Then there is a rhapsody over Prof. Churchill's rendering of the "Trial Scene in Pickwick" in seminary hall. The lavish use of adjectives does not sound out of date to-day. We should draw on our stock of superlatives just the same if we could hear him now.

Then, O girls, do you remember the night when the barn just north of the seminary burned down? The long bell was rung,—the bell that only warned of great events, like meteoric showers or changing rooms,—and we were advised to put on our wraps, and betake ourselves with our pails to the scene of action. We formed a double line from the bathrooms to the north wing door, and thence to the fence. In the weird, flaring light, the waterproofed figures, in all stages of coiffure and dishevelment, passing pails up and down as rhythmically, if not as silently, as in a gymnastic drill, must have been ludicrous enough, but we were too much absorbed to realize it at the time. A parody on Tennyson's "Light Brigade" was the most popular composition read in our division that week.

This reminds one of the new *régime* inaugurated by Miss Holmes that year, of senior composition readings in the seminary hall, in the evening, with concomitants of music and dancing—I mean music and flowers—and invitations to privileged sections or classes. Then, we considered it a charming arrangement for all but the readers. Now, alas! it is sad to reflect that the invited listeners may have been the chief victims.

Miss Holmes' method of book-keeping in those days would not have borne investigation. Her debit and credit account with her division put all the credit on our side, and our dues were never set down. We could have made her account-book tell a different story, with the balance on the other side.

Then there come some quotations from an address of Dr. Kirk's;—and we almost see again the stately figure, erect even when groping his way to the door, and needing the assistance of a hand up the platform steps,—manly and direct in his utterances, and helpful always.

Further back in the record, following some lively remarks on Monday's Bible lessons and baked beans, is a brief mention of "a young man from Chicago, a teacher of a large Bible class there, who spoke to us at devotions. He was certainly very much in earnest, but his grammar was embarrassing." If the girl's prophetic soul could have foreseen Mr. Moody's future career, she might not have disposed of him in such summary fashion.

But, after all, the best can never come to the surface in such memories. The tenderest and deepest thoughts of love and gratitude are awakened by such insignificant sentences as this: "M. and A. were at recess meeting to-night"—"Spent time last evening with K"—"Miss B. came in to say good-night after the tardy"—mere hints of loving companionships, of helpful words spoken at the right time, that have influenced all after living, for many a one of us. With every page we turn, we say with fresh gratitude, "God bless our *alma mater!*" She helped to develop not only mind, but character. That is one reason for our trust in her. God bless her evermore!

LETTER FROM MISS JESSUP, '47.

ASSOCIATE PRINCIPAL, 1855-62.

WESTERN FEMALE SEMINARY, OXFORD, O., June, 1887.

To the Alumnæ of Mt. Holyoke Seminary,—Sisters, Daughters, Beloved Friends:—

THESE terms express what you were to me during the fifteen years of my residence at the seminary; also what you have been during the nearly thirty years of my infirmity since; for my connection with *alma mater* has been continued, although I have not seen her face since my departure in 1860. Not a journal record, not a full published description of any passing anniversary, has failed to be sent to me, with all interesting published accounts of each passing occasion of general interest as it occurred. The different class-letters, too, have kept you individually in mind, and made me acquainted with your service and devotion to our common Lord.

The tie which binds the alumnæ of these Mt. Holyoke schools is the family tie,—strengthened by many cords, the central and strongest being that which binds to Christ and his church. And this explains the deep mutual interest and the common devotion to our *alma mater*.

It was Christ in Mary Lyon and his work through her and her co-laborers that has made Mt. Holyoke Seminary the efficient agency she has been for the elevation of woman in this and other lands. Let us bring all our trophies and lay them at his blessed feet, and give to him all the praise, which is his due. In this way shall we most truly honor the seminary and its sainted founders. For Christ and his church let each Mt. Holyoke daughter live, labor, and suffer if need be, and thus will the mission of the seminary be attained.

Allow me to express my gratitude to you collectively for the honor you have put upon the institution by your benevolent and consecrated lives. Also to the many friends who have so often expressed their personal sympathy and affection during these years of helpless infirmity and trial. Let me however assure you that it has been good for me to have been afflicted. In no other way could I so well have learned the lessons of trust and deep experience as this. Romans 5: 1-6 explains what I would say. Peace with God through our Lord Jesus Christ and hope which maketh not ashamed are for us all, yet some of us have need of the tribulation to enter fully into them.

Hoping to meet you all at the blessed reunion, when our Lord shall call us to the heavenly home,

Yours in his name,   EMILY JESSUP.

LETTER FROM MISS ELLIS, '55.

ASSOCIATE PRINCIPAL, 1867-72.

To the Dear Mt. Holyoke Family, this day assembled, Greetings:—

MY heart almost fails me as I attempt to comply with Mrs. Gulliver's request to write a few words for you at this family gathering. I sympathize here with the many, many others who are detained from going up to the great convocation. "Tis a great sorrow to me, for I have looked forward to this event, not months, but years; there are so many of you whom I wanted to see once more—classmates, teachers, associates and pupils,—a great army. In my wanderings I have met many whom I had never seen within Holyoke's walls. You, too, I should like to meet again. All this denied me, if I could only have one glimpse of you all, it would be an inspiration, greater even than that which came to me twenty-five years ago, when I looked into the faces of those who had graduated before me. I saw in those faces that which told me of earnest lives, and true work for God, for country, and for all in need. It seemed to me then that I had never seen a more noble looking assembly, and I never had.

A little more than half a century ago a noted foreigner came to these United States to investigate the political and social institutions of the country. After all his observations, he said to a friend, "If I were asked to what the singular prosperity and growing strength of the American people ought mainly to be attributed, I should reply, 'To the superiority of their women.'"

To-day we celebrate the fiftieth birthday of this institution, founded by a woman who saw the growing needs of her country and the world, the work which woman must do in the coming years, and the necessity for school homes where young women might secure the preparation which would properly fit them for the work so speedily to open before them.

Mt. Holyoke Seminary was not opened one month too soon, and with the similar institutions which owe their existence to Mary Lyon's foresight, energy, and eager desire for the extension of Christ's kingdom, it has proved to the world that the higher education of woman makes her a greater power in securing the "prosperity and strength" of her own country and in uplifting the world.

If De Tocqueville, to-day, could revisit us, would not his confidence in the superiority of American women be strengthened and deepened? Would he not look with admiring eyes on the work which is now being done for them?

How many besides those who call Mt. Holyoke Seminary *alma mater* thank God that he raised up Mary Lyon for the work which she has accomplished for them! As for ourselves we know that our lives, and the world, and heaven, yea all things are more to us than if we had not enjoyed what she prepared for us.

With gratitude to the many who in the long, weary months of the last four years have not failed to remember me in your prayers, and with love to all,

I am yours in the bonds of *alma mater*, MARY ELLIS.

LETTER FROM MISS PEABODY, '48.

PRINCIPAL WESTERN SEMINARY, OXFORD, O.

To the Alumnæ of Mt. Holyoke Seminary in Convention at the old place on the Semi-Centennial Anniversary, June 22, 1887, Greetings and Congratulations:—

GREETINGS because we are of the same family; congratulations because you are present while some of us who desire to be among the favored are held at our posts. We should not be true daughters of Mary Lyon if we deserted our work even for this joyful reunion. But there will be another gathering day, when we hope not one will fail to respond to the roll call.

Some one has said that a system is not to be judged by the men who made it, but by the men it makes. Others may judge of the success of Mary Lyon's system of education by the kind of women it has made, but for a moment let me dwell on the principles that have made these women. Miss Lyon was eminently a woman of principles. Well do some of us remember how often we were confronted at the afternoon hall exercise with, "Young ladies, I have a great principle to give you to-day." If the principles of action are right the concrete will be. "Dare to be right" was her motto. "Make a thing right first and be content to wait for it to become popular." "Do not look for praise or pay." "Love must be the constraining motive; love that gives and forgets self." "Many fields will remain waste and unfruitful if not cultivated for love; love like that which brought Christ from heaven to earth." "Do not wait to do some great thing. You may never have the chance or the ability." "Be willing to do a little thing. Do not think that we place your expenses so low to save your father's money for your selfish indulgence. Oh no! We hope rather by this means to place you under such obligations that you will gladly do the same for others."

One incident which will be remembered by the representatives of the fall of 1848 will illustrate her power to make self-sacrifice for the general good not only attractive but desirable. The scene was the seminary hall: over two hundred girls were in their seats; Miss Whitman on the platform was arranging the laundry circles; one of the limited number of hours was very inconvenient and no one would volunteer to take it. After a few fruitless efforts at persuasion, Miss Whitman laid down pencil and paper, left the hall for a moment and, returning with Miss Lyon, surrendered the field to her. With a beaming face, as if she had come to make an announcement that she expected would be received with enthusiasm, Miss Lyon gave a two minutes' talk upon the reflex as well as direct advantages to character of every opportunity for subordinating personal preference to the general good, and said, " Now those who would like " (her favorite way of putting the question) " to be arranged for this less desirable hour, may rise." In an instant all were on their feet. Accepting gracefully the willingness of all for the present sacrifice, with equal tact and honest wisdom she persuaded all but about thirty to forego the present opportunity and wait for the next chance for similar self-improvement.

Miss Lyon sleeps, but her principles, drawn from the word of God, and especially from the life and example of Christ, will never sleep. May her successors steadfastly continue to hold the school to its original principles!

With love to all and especially to those between '45 and '53,
  Yours in the tie that binds,

            HELEN PEABODY.

ANNUAL MEETING OF THE ALUMNÆ ASSOCIATION.
WEDNESDAY, 2 P. M.

THE afternoon meeting was opened with singing by the Seminary Quartette. Prayer was offered by Mrs. Frisbee (Eliza C. Haskell, '56). The minutes of the last annual meeting were read by the secretary, Miss Louise F. Cowles, '66. The president, Mrs. Moses Smith (Emily A. White, '58), called on Mrs. Fairchild of New Haven (Thera West, '61), to give some account of the origin of the Association, who said in substance :—

At an informal meeting in 1871, where Miss Evans gave an inspiring talk suggesting what the alumnæ might do for *alma mater*, a few New Haven ladies were present. They went home and called together all in their vicinity who had attended school here, prepared circulars and sent them throughout the state of Connecticut. Though no state organization was effected, a local association was soon after formed in New Haven. At the meeting of the American Board in that city, the following year, a large and enthusiastic company of graduates and others, having met for the purpose, formed the National Association of Holyoke Alumnæ, and Mrs. Moses Smith was made president; Miss Harriet N. Haskell, '55, and Miss Victoria A. White, '71, corresponding secretaries ; Miss Mary F. Mather, '56, recording secretary; and Miss Sarah H. Melvin, '62, treasurer.

Other items are added from Holyoke Alumnæ Associations, a paper prepared by Sarah A. Clarke, '79, of New Haven :—

On the afternoon of the thirty-fourth anniversary, July 6, 1871, about seventy alumnæ, representing twenty-four different classes, besides a number who were not graduates, met in the seminary library—since converted into the lecture room—to discuss methods of aiding *alma mater*. Miss Spofford, associate principal 1852-55, presided. In the course of their deliberations the venerable Dr. Kirk, then almost blind, was led into the room. After inquiring with paternal interest about the location and work of so many present who were once students here, his thoughts turned upon the subject of prayer, whose power he said was almost as unknown to the world at large as the power of steam was in his boyhood. He believed that if the band of women in that room were united in prayer for the conversion of the world, Satan's kingdom would soon fall. His words led all present to take new interest in the Saturday evening concert of prayer for each other and for our own and the kindred seminaries.

Miss Evans, who had gone from Mt. Holyoke to the seminary at Painesville too recently to need formal introduction by Miss Spofford, urged the propriety of rendering material aid, and proposed organized effort in procuring funds and appliances adequate to the wants of the seminary. "We all know," said she, "what the alumni of Amherst, Harvard, and Yale are doing. And some of us remember the good work that secured the blessing of steam-heating to our institution ; how interested we were in it, and how we rejoiced as day after day for sixteen weeks every mail brought us larger or smaller contributions for the cause." [It deserves to be recorded that Miss Evans was herself one of the prime movers and most efficient workers in that great effort for steam-heating.]

Two of the New Haven ladies who listened to Miss Evans that day and resolved to act upon her suggestion, were Mrs. Fairchild of '61, and Mrs. Cora Welch Millingen of '59. Twenty ladies soon after met by invitation at the house of Mrs. Fairchild, and the New Haven Association organized with Mrs. Fairchild president, and Mrs. Millingen secretary. Their constitution was the basis of that adopted by the National Association formed the next year, and by the local branches afterward. The object of all is "to promote the prosperity of the seminary in recognition of its claims upon the gratitude of the students who have received from it so freely ; to seek to bring together in social reunion former members of the seminary and to incite all to increased devotion to the service of Christ."

Holyoke gatherings continue in connection with the meetings of the American Board, but since its first year the National Association has held its annual meetings at the seminary, anniversary week. By an article inserted in the constitution in 1874, "the treasurer and the recording secretary must be elected from the members of the faculty resident at the seminary." On the resignation of Miss Mather at that time, Miss Lucy J. Holmes, '58, was chosen recording secretary and filled the office for ten years, when she resigned, and Miss Louise F. Cowles, '66, was elected.

Officers are elected biennially. Presidents of the several branches are vice-presidents, *ex officio*, of the National Association. Each branch has its own method of conducting meetings, combining literary entertainment with social festivities. Membership in a branch, by the annual payment of $1.00, constitutes membership in the National Association.

At the annual meetings of the latter a record of the reported marriages and deaths is read, recognition is made of the daughters of alumnæ in school, and generally some literary entertainment is furnished by the class that meets then for its twenty-fifth anniversary since graduation.

It has been repeatedly proposed to unite the Memorandum Society with the Alumnæ Association, the membership of the two organizations being practically the same. But since the work of the one is that of the mother following with interest her absent daughters, and of the other that of the daughters seeking to aid the mother, it has been thought hitherto that the two objects could be accomplished better by co-operation than by union.

TREASURER'S REPORT.

SARAH H. MELVIN, '62.

The cash receipts of the treasurer in these fifteen years amount to $35,095.67—of which $28,350 belongs to the Mary Lyon fund; $1,869.00 was given towards building and furnishing Williston Hall; $1,103.50 for the mineralogical and geological cabinets; $1,145.00 for the educational fund; $365.00 from the Boston and Worcester Alumnæ Associations, for microscopes; $500 in one donation for the greenhouse; $500 in another for improvements in the seminary hall; $500 was received from a legacy of Effie McKennan.

Though the Tolman fund of about $4,000.00, the income of which is designed for the benefit of weary teachers, did not come into our treasury, it should be mentioned here.

Besides these gifts of money, there have been numerous and valuable gifts from individuals and classes of which a grateful record is kept with names of donors. These have not only aided in filling the cabinets and art gallery of Williston Hall and furnishing its various departments, but have also contributed in many ways to the comfort and enjoyment of the household. The estimated value of gifts from classes alone is not less than $4,000.00. Our missionary alumnæ have kept us in constant remembrance by their gifts, of which may be mentioned rare and costly antiquities from various lands; while in the department of natural science, from China, Ceylon, Persia, Palestine, Turkey, Spain, Africa, Labrador, and some of our North American Indian missions, many valuable collections of plants, woods, and seeds have been received through their means, as well as birds, serpents, fishes, shells, insects, horns and skins of quadrupeds from Africa; shells, birds, and minerals from India, shells and corals from the Marshall and Hawaiian Islands; and the same from Burma, China, and Japan.

REPORTS FROM BRANCH ASSOCIATIONS.

NEW HAVEN ASSOCIATION.—Mrs. Fairchild: As a representative of the New Haven Association I cannot report large numbers, nor large gifts. But in the matter of quality we can stand with the rest of you, for some of our members were here in the very earliest days and both learned and taught under Miss Lyon. Our first secretary occupies a position in Constantinople as wife of the professor of literature in Robert College. Our first treasurer is in Africa. Our second treasurer is in India. We often speak of our privilege as solicitors. I hope this privilege has been embraced by all those present. If any one here does not know that it is a privilege, we rejoice to assure her of the fact.

HARTFORD ASSOCIATION.—Mrs. W. W. Woodworth (Lydia A. Sessions, '56) said that that Association was organized a year ago last May. One of its officers gave the first five hundred dollars to the Mary Lyon fund.

BOSTON ASSOCIATION.—Miss Emma Ditto, '61, of Dana Hall, Wellesley: It gives me great pleasure to represent the Boston alumnæ and to bring their greetings, their congratulations, and their hopes for Mt. Holyoke Seminary; first, congratulations that we have raised the fund, and second, that we raised it slowly and with hard work. It is of the goodness of God that it has come with patience, prayer, self-abnegation, and through the felicities of soliciting. Every one of us that has shared that opportunity should rejoice and be glad. We are sharing in the pain that Mary Lyon suffered when she went about taking ten-cent subscriptions. We find ourselves in the same line of work. When other institutions get hundreds of thousands of dollars our dear school does not get ten thousand. This is strange when we know that here they make money go farthest, that they quietly transmute gold into that higher wisdom beyond the price of rubies, into character, intellect, heart. About Easter time, when the money was creeping in slowly, one, two, five, ten dollars, and it stood still on the thirteenth thousand, I went into my closet one Sunday morning and shut one of those blessed doors that we have shut many a time. Then I saw that we had to get this money slowly, because God had a greater blessing to give with it, the trial of the faith being more precious than the money. The money came by prayer and self-sacrifice. It is sacred money. We are holding to the principles in which Mary Lyon laid this institution. It must reach the highest in character, and it must extend to the greatest number. Mt. Holyoke Seminary first and foremost stands for Christ, and the round world knows it. There is no need of saying that it is orthodox; oh no, that spells itself. Its first aim is to link the intellect and the soul to God through Christ. This being done it is content to be plain. Sometimes the only way to be distinguished is not to be distinguished. Mt. Holyoke has held to her principles and that is great cause for congratulation. Our hopes are in the same line. Let us be more faithful in our work and prayer and more willing to do everything that we can possibly do for our school.

PACIFIC ASSOCIATION.—Mrs. Mills of Mills College (Susan L. Tolman, '45): When I was a little girl my father said that he wanted all his daughters to be educated at Mount Holyoke, and first and last we were here twenty-five years. Of the six thus taught only two are living, and one of those two greets you from the Pacific coast. The other is thinking of us, and my heart has been going across the continent as well as to that great cloud of witnesses who have washed their robes and made them white in the blood of the Lamb. I have come to bring you the greeting of the Association of the Pacific. It was organized last April when Miss Shattuck was with us. We are scattered from British Columbia to Mexico. We cannot often come together, but this year about forty gathered at Mills Seminary. The alumnæ of that institution asked if they could not be counted as grandchildren, and they send their greeting. Our Association met and I was elected president, Miss Emily S. Wilson, '62, vice-president, and Mrs. Jewett (Alice Dwinell, '72), secretary. Miss Allie R. Bills, '67, is our treasurer. The teachers from here have done good work there. You can hardly appreciate the good they have done. Some have labored as home missionaries and some as teachers, and all are loyal to Mt. Holyoke. It was our desire and prayer that we might contribute something to this fund. A thousand dollars had been consecrated to it by one who had said when near death, "Don't forget the thousand for Ceylon, the thousand for Williams, and the thousand for Holyoke." To the five hundred from the Association is added this thousand from my husband. We wish it were a great deal more. Many think of the people of California as rich, but the money is not in the hands of those who have consecrated their lives to Christ as Mary Lyon did.

I was interested in the remarks of a California lady of culture who attended the Centennial Exposition and studied the various school exhibits. She was highly educated. I asked her about the result of her investigations and she said: "There are two schools that have done the best work." I replied, "One is Mt. Holyoke, I know!" The other was Oberlin. I was glad to hear Miss Ditto say that the word Mt. Holyoke means orthodox, and consecrated to Christ. May every daughter of Holyoke learn to freely give as she has freely received!

I bring you a greeting from Miss Jessup, for I turned aside to see her. She said: "The time of release is close at hand. The deformities are soon to be covered with the white robes." I spent a Sunday with her, and came away with a feeling of gratitude that I can work, but thankful that I had talked with one who is already reflecting the light from above. I wish some token of our love and sympathy might be sent her. [She was remembered by several classes.]

ASSOCIATION OF THE NORTHWEST.—Mrs. Nichols of Chicago (Mary Foster, '56): Our mother said when we went forth, "If ye bend not to this work heart and hand and brain, ye shall live your lives in vain." And so we have been busy, very busy all these years. This is quite true, no doubt, of all of us, but we think it is specially true of the branch of the Northwest, which, in the absence of our president, Miss Merrick of Chicago, I have the honor to represent. Now, as in the earlier days, the most enterprising people who wish to find a way to express their indomitable energy, go West. A large number of these when they reach Chicago, where people have to rush with the rush or be run over, find the atmosphere congenial, at least stimulating, and make the city their home. Shall I tell you the kind of work they do? A few years ago the Woman's Board of the Interior convened in Rockford, Ill. The presiding officer was complimented by everybody and especially by one doctor of divinity, in such terms as these, "Not one minister in a hundred could preside over such a meeting with such skill, tact, and quiet dignity." This presiding officer was one of our alumnæ. The other day I took up a copy of the *Interior*, a prominent religious paper published in Chicago, and read as follows :—

"We earnestly and respectfully suggest that hereafter no commissioner be eligible to the moderatorship of our General Assembly who cannot present a duly attested certificate that he has attended a meeting of our

Woman's Presbyterian Board of Missions of the Northwest and carefully observed the manner in which its model president, Mrs. Douglass of Chicago, conducts the business of that board. She never loses her head; she is always master of the situation; she never takes hand or eye off the machine, and she always sees that it turns out a first-class article of business straight along from morning to night, without stoppages or splurges. If she could only once be moderator of our Assembly she would shorten its sessions one-third and leave useful practical lessons behind her." She is another of our alumnæ.

A little church in one of the suburbs is without a pastor. One woman, by her prayers and efforts, secures a minister and does more to keep that church alive than all the rest of the church together, and she also is one of our alumnæ. Were you on the ground you could find examples like this any day. Of course the younger and prettier go off like hot cakes in the matrimonial market, and it is but just to say that the Mt. Holyoke trained husbands are the best kind of husbands. And their children are the model trained children of the world. A few of us started out to devote our lives to something outside of matrimony and, I must say, resisted the most persevering appeals till some ardent suitor, who was bound to fight it out on that line, put in the plea that Providence favored his suit, and the happy homes that have been the result have justified the persevering appeals. There is one thing that puzzles us. We have always been taught that the counterfeit proves the genuine, but with us there are no counterfeits. All whom we have met in Chicago of our Israel are Israelites indeed. We take credit to ourselves, though this may not sound very modest, that we set the ball rolling which resulted in the election of women on our board of trustees. We are unquestionably loyal to *alma mater* and wear the title, "daughters of Holyoke," as proudly as queens their crowns, and no British sovereign celebrating her half-century of royalty can receive more loyal pledges of love than we bring here to-day.

THE PHILADELPHIA ASSOCIATION.—Mrs. Evans (Laura J. Snow, '64): The Association of Philadelphia, organized a year ago last February, is due to the zeal of Mrs. McFarland, the president, and Mrs. Nelson of Westchester. It is different from the New England associations in being composed of the younger graduates, teachers, who come as missionaries, to bring the evangel of sweetness and light to our somewhat benighted country, compared with New England. Besides these we have with us Mrs. Webb of the class of '44 and her sister, Miss Foote, who was formerly a teacher here. From them we learn about the "good old times," those hard old times, we should think. Then there are some among us who have done nothing but train children and husbands and servants. But our husbands are good and are well trained.

I think it is rather hard that our little association—of only forty-five—should be brought out after these other corner-stones, so much larger and so much more highly polished than we. But we have large plans for the future, and shall get new inspiration from this visit. I think we shall go home with brighter fires on our altars and shall let it be known farther and wider in that region that there is a Mt. Holyoke and that it is a good place for training women. We feel the responsibility of our heritage in Miss Lyon's labors and prayers. Pennsylvania has a share in it in Bryn Mawr College. When I go there and see the abundant appliances furnished that college at its beginning, I covet similar abundance for *alma mater;* but, as has been said, it is good to gain slowly, and to gain the fruits of toil and prayer.

THE ASSOCIATION OF NEW YORK AND BROOKLYN.—Miss Mary Brigham of '48, of Brooklyn Heights Seminary: The blessing of work as a bond of union has been wonderfully exemplified in the history of the New York and Brooklyn Association, which we organized a year ago last February. We began immediately with the thought that we must work for the Mary Lyon fund. I am glad to be able to stand as the representative of that delightful association of women. I am honored by being invited to do it, and I am proud of the Association. I have a right to speak of them, not because they have elected me as president, but because I was the teacher of many of them and am one of the veterans in the service. We number more than one hundred; almost every age is represented, from one member of the class of '39 that Miss Lyon used to call her twelve disciples, down to one of the sweet girl graduates of '86. We have a strong hold upon the seminary, for each link is attached to one preceding, so that we go back to Mary Lyon. I am very glad to bring the greeting from so many hearts, not only to the seminary, but to this great company of ladies, feeling that we and you are bound together not only by ties of love for this beautiful seminary,—for to me it grows more beautiful every year,—but by our hopes of what it shall be in the future. My heart is full of it. I desire to see it not only a seminary, but to make it a college in the strictest sense of the word. Great wisdom will be necessary to adjust all the peculiar matters and circumstances and conditions; but I believe that in the trustees and faculty there is abundant wisdom, and if we go on and work and labor for our beloved *alma mater* as we may and ought, if we take the privilege of solicitors and use it to its full measure, we may live to see the day when this shall be one of the leading colleges of the land.

THE FRANKLIN COUNTY ASSOCIATION.—Miss Emily C. Graves, '61, Greenfield: In behalf of our association formed only six months ago, I bring you the cordial greetings of Franklin county, the home of Miss Lyon and Miss Fiske, a county which has furnished the seminary with over two hundred and twenty pupils and ten teachers. At our last meeting one member was from the class of '86, and another was here the day before the seminary was opened and assisted Deacon Safford and Mrs. Montague in cleaning the windows. Our contribution has been small, but we hope for larger results in the future.

ASSOCIATION IN THE HAWAIIAN ISLANDS.—Martha J. Chamberlain, '53, of Honolulu, spoke in behalf of the association, as follows: *Aloha oe!* I love you! This salutation that I bring you from daughters far away has a tenderness in it that you can hardly know. It is the filial greeting of hearts that longed to respond to the call and be here with us to-day. Organized in 1880, and but sixteen in number, we are the least of all the societies, but we are thoroughly loyal.

From Mrs. Sophie Smith Burt, I bear especial messages to the later alumnæ. In the right time and place you shall hear them with the particulars of her shipwreck and the rescue. She has come among us to be a great blessing. *Aloha!*

The hymn, "My faith looks up to thee," was sung.

WORCESTER ASSOCIATION.—Mrs. Baldwin (Ella L. T. Peckham, '67): At our organization in the Salem Street Church, Worcester, in 1875, Miss Ward and Miss Shattuck met forty of us who reside in or near the city, representing nearly every Holyoke class. Since that time, we keep on our lists the name of every one in our vicinity who has studied here, and remind her of our meetings spring and fall. Though these gatherings are well attended, not all our seventy members can always be present. When the prospective branch in Providence is formed it will lessen the attendance we have had from Rhode Island.

We aimed to raise five hundred dollars for the Mary Lyon fund, but, with the help of one hundred dollars from E. A. Goodnow, Esq., and two hundred from Mr. G. Henry Whitcomb, two friends whom we are pleased to number among our honorary members, we are enabled to make the sum one thousand dollars.

It has been said that Massachusetts has never taken the interest in this institution that might be expected, and I suggest the question whether the state could not rightfully be called upon to aid us.

Our president, Mrs. Judge Dewey (Sarah A. B. Tufts of '42), was a pupil of Miss Lyon. It seems to me that a few weeks with her must have been equal to a full course in these later days. If ever the seminary has a new name I hope it will be "The Mary Lyon College."

AMHERST ASSOCIATION.—Mrs. Wm. A. Magill (Matilda W. Smith, '58): I represent the youngest branch, our organization having been formed last month, largely through the influence of Mrs. Thompson (Esther Munsell, '59). Our twenty members represent the seminary from 1845 to 1885. Though young and small we are rapidly growing vigorous and mean to do our part in good time.

REMINISCENCES.

MISS CHARLOTTE MORRILL, '61, BROOKLYN, N. Y.

THE virtues once held a meeting on Mount Olympus. It is quite safe to say here that they were all women, and you can readily imagine with what enthusiasm and expressions of delight they threw themselves into each other's arms. There were, however, two who had never met before, and who asked a mutual introduction. They were Benevolence and Gratitude. They have seldom met since, but they meet here to-day. If you reflect upon how great a gulf is fixed between the senior and junior classes, you may perhaps comprehend my amazement when a member of the class of '58, that senior class who still have a halo about their heads, asked me, a junior of the same year, to give to-day some memories of the far-away school days. My gratitude and surprise at so unexpected an honor were so overwhelming that I feared I might be like a good Methodist sister, who was asked in prayer-meeting to tell an experience she could never forget. After two or three repetitions of her inability to forget it, she dropped into her seat, exclaiming, "but it is entirely gone from me at this moment." Yet who can forget her junior year at Mt. Holyoke? Then the summer mornings were full of singing birds always waiting outside the window to help us begin the day with happiness. Personal rheumatism was unknown; insomnia had not been invented, we walked without fatigue, we ran and were not weary. Then all was gold that glittered—then we were young.

In 1858 there came a verdant trembling maiden from Vermont. She was provided with clothing suitable for the season and climate, including flannels, woolen hose, thick shoes, overshoes, leggins, also an umbrella; provided also with a good knowledge of English grammar, modern geography, readiness in mental arithmetic and Latin grammar, and with a check for $40 payable strictly in advance. She passed her examinations, shed the usual homesick tears, fell to scouring knives with neatness, dispatch, a potato, and Bristol brick, and was compelled to take a rapid review of Nepos. No castle, no, not even one in Spain, ever looked higher or more formidable than did Mt. Holyoke Seminary on the evening of September 22. I rode up from the ferry in one of the landaus peculiar to South Hadley, and in company with some of the senior class. I have seen kings and queens, presidents, justices of the peace, church ushers and hotel clerks, but never such dignity as sat upon these seniors. I felt unworthy to enter by the same door that they did, and looked askance at the south front door. That door is the only false thing I ever found at Mt. Holyoke. I shouldn't speak of it now only that fifty years and false fronts seem to belong to the same head.

One of the great pleasures of our quarter-century class-meeting of last year was that Miss Chapin was here to welcome us. She kindly told us some of her early experiences here, and we appreciated, as we could not in our school days, the great debt Mt. Holyoke owes to her. While I do not forget her great executive ability, her suavity of manner and her universal sympathy, I remember also how acceptable her quick appreciation of fun was to us. I know she will pardon me if I recall here how a conscientious and tormented schoolmate gave as a criticism, "Noise after the retiring bell." Miss Chapin asked us to "rise, young ladies." Then she commenced: "If you were not disturbed more than one night during the past week,"—" more than two," and so on to seven. Still the author of the criticism stood with Spartan firmness, until Miss Chapin said: "This is sad. This young lady has been disturbed more than seven nights the past week." The memory of the sparkle in her eyes and the hasty sitting down has resisted twenty-five years of the corroding tooth of time.

Who does not remember Miss Jessup! I know and feel how many corners of my single acre are untilled, but I record here to-day that her life has been a constant inspiration to me. I have seen a great deal of poor building, of thin walls and slender foundations, and have loved to think how she placed the granite and built slowly but built for all time. Grand in her life, grand in her patient long-suffering, I write her name as the name of one who has overcome the world. I made up a great deal of minus time in her society that junior year. How many times she has asked me to step from her room to the basement with a bowl, and how glad I was to step anywhere with anything! Dr. Beecher said the doctrine of the perseverance of the saints never troubled him, but the perseverance of the sinners did. Miss Jessup could sympathize with him that year of '58. There was a coterie of girls who early and late, in season and out of season, devoted themselves to mischief and kept her busy setting traps. As it was not at all a case of setting a rogue to catch a rogue, many of the traps were set in paths the girls did not frequent, but when one did slip in she never forgot it. Oh that No. 108 and that closet and the crushing humility one felt when she emerged! Nell Swett said she never waited to open the door but always slipped out through the keyhole.

On a fair white page of memory's tablet I read the names of the blessed dead. With loving hands I throw over their graves the flowers of grateful affection. Through misty eyes I see written the dear names of Catharine Hopkins, Sara A. Start, Mary F. Stearns (my patient, long-suffering section teacher), and Julia M. Tolman. They have not been immortalized in verse or enshrined in marble, but the memory of the just, always blessed, is theirs, and their names need neither song nor chisel to make them more illustrious.

Last year I walked into the seminary hall, and I saw with these very eyes girls sitting on the platform. I saw among them (I know this will tax the credulity of the older graduates) a live man. A violin materialized before me and my amazed ears heard classic music. Like an attenuated and most ghostly ghost the concert singing of '58 appeared to me. I wonder if I am the only woman here who feels a twinge as I call the name of Lucinda D. Hodge. Twenty-six years have passed since she joined the choir of the invisible and speedily forgot the petty stings and tormenting ways of the careless but not unkind choir visible. Long before this we cannot doubt that the discords of her life like the discords of our music have faded, and the divine sunlight has lifted the last shadow from her sad heart.

In that corner of the garden of my memory where the forget-me-nots turn their sweet blue eyes upon me, and the star of Bethlehem raises its radiant white head, I read written in flowers the name of Lydia W. Shattuck. From the same garden I pluck the laurel-leaves, and, with an affection that increases as the years go by, I crown the names which still glow with loving light, the beloved names of Mary A. Brigham, Mary Ellis, Helen M. French, Harriet Sessions, Julia E. Ward.

I feel my lips grow white and my knees grow weak as I come back to that senior class again! The world has never seen any other such corner-stones. Think of a class that has furnished Mt. Holyoke seminary with a principal and seven teachers, the Woman's Board of the Interior and our National Alumnæ Association with a president! The æsthetic department here is a *Noble* monument to '58. I knew the path to the front seat intimately, but I never found seniors there. When Thursday blazed with those serried columns : absence from church ; absence from school exercises ; absence from table ; absence from domestic work ; and so on to speaking in public sleeping places, their ranks were never broken. They sat in solemn silence polished after the similitude of a palace. They were adepts in the art of whispering in the hall. They would not have thrown even a molecule from the windows. Their wardrobes knew not the word disorder ; their account books, like their owners, never lost their balance. They carried no fire ; their lamps never went out for lack of oil, but always out of proper respect for the retiring bell. They were never taken by the throat and compelled to pay their debts. If their extra work happened to be floor cleaning, they always conveyed the mop on a line exactly tallying with the grain of the wood. They never interpolated the room regulations. You would never have found in a senior room the sentence to avoid lighting matches on the wall made to read : " To avoid lighting on the wall," and, though you sought diligently, there could never, never be found the direction to keep the bellows in the closet metamorphosed into "to keep the fellows in the closet"! They made a mark everywhere except upon the building. The most alluring eatable never tempted them to a purchase. No first, second, or evil communications ever corrupted their good manners. No other class ever had Nell Swett, who has mitigated the climate of New Jersey, and whose wit has cured more dyspepsia than the mental healers, Christian scientists, and all other heretics. When some feminine Oliver Twist asked for more heat in the dining room, and Miss Jessup assured us that nothing was necessary so that the young ladies were properly protected, and Nell came down to dinner with more wrapping than was taken off Rameses II., explaining that she was only properly protected, even Miss Jessup could not refrain from laughing at the grotesque and many colored figure.

I must not dwell longer upon the virtues and graces of this monumental class. If they should be written, every one, I suppose that even the world itself could not contain the books that should be written.

Our New York New England Society gives an annual dinner at Delmonico's that they may keep themselves in lively remembrance of the style of living of our Pilgrim forefathers. As I see the steam-heating apparatus, know of the artesian well, ride in the elevator, visit the art rooms, enter the library, look over the grounds, I feel that I owe a debt to the present students of Mt. Holyoke. If time allowed I would harrow their youthful ears and draw floods of tears from their bright young eyes as I narrated the rigors of a quarter century since. I wonder if these pampered young ladies ever saw a Franklin stove, an instrument of torture which sent heat into the chimney and deposited the smoke in the room. I am bound to say that, as I have sat shivering by registers, which always seem like a memorial tablet that ought to be inscribed "Sacred to the memory of a departed fire," I have wished for a Franklin stove, and felt that I would cheerfully lift and carry one end of the wood basket for the luxury of an open wood fire.

The second year of the course I spent in maturing. However I may have forgotten the work of the other years, I have kept right on practicing that of '58-'59. The studies are hardly within my memory at all. I am taking up *De Senectute* again, and I find many new wrinkles in it. My herbarium is but a little faded flower. The Brooklyn people are always studying bridges. I have forgotten what the *pons asinorum* connects and whether it be suspended or built on piers. Geology still interests me. I am on the most familiar terms with fossils and on the lookout for footprints, particularly those of the crow. Of ecclesiastical history, I recall only the picture of St. Lawrence on his gridiron, and remember how at recitations I frequently envied his comparative comfort. Some of you heard me say this last year, but I found I had put the picture in the wrong book. I gave it to Paley's Natural Theology. I return it now to its native Marsh.

I drop from view the middle year, the chrysalis state when one is neither caterpillar nor butterfly, and hasten on to the senior year. At last we reached that serene height. We despised the juniors, and patronized the middlers. We began to have views. We felt that the world was hardly worthy of us. We sat opposite at table. We led in domestic work. We held class meetings which we thought would revolutionize the world. We quarreled over a class ring. We were the pioneers—*horresco referens*—of the class album! We walked to church and took our diplomas just as forty-eight other classes have done.

A drunken man strayed into a church where the clergyman preached in the pointed style. When he exclaimed, "Where is the drunkard?" the inebriated man rose and stood till that line of remark was exhausted. Then the good man called out, "And where is the hypocrite?" The interloper leaned forward, tapped the deacon on the shoulder and said, "Get up! I stood when I was called." When I ask where is the princess of room-mates,—she who was good but not goody-good; she who took in one black sheep after another, and treated each one as if she were white; she of whom all the black sheep spoke well, kept ever for her a warm corner of the heart, and were never quite so black again; she whose quiet, unconscious influence has been and is still a power in the world,—you should see standing Elizabeth B. Prentiss. In 1886, twenty-five of us came back home, and I closed the class roll again. I spare you to-day any repetitions of the memories I gave then. I will not produce these fragments and, as in my youth I sometimes did, set before you a dish of variety. I omitted one very important item last year. We were the war class. We were here when Democracy fell into its twenty-four years' sleep. We recall President Buchanan's administration, which he closed by proclaiming a fast, leading Bayard Taylor to say, this kind goeth not out but by fasting and prayer. It passes wonder with me that General Grant failed to mention in his account of the civil war, and that the Century in its many war histories has also forgotten, the case of blue and red needle-books sent by the class of '61 to the Northern army. Doubtless much of the success of our armies was due to this offering on the altar of our native land; for surely in the midst of carnage, when bullets are flying and shells are bursting, the nerves must become steel, courage must rise to its utmost, when a soldier reflects that he has with him either a red or a blue needle-book.

I know that the president will extinguish me with a tardy bell unless I hasten to my farewell. Since it has been given to others to recount the memories of the sacred hours, the holy, happy memories that hold Mt. Holyoke far above the world and crown her with celestial light, I may not even mention how I treasure them. As I go from these heavenly places back to the murky atmosphere of the great world lying in wickedness away from the green grass and violets, back to brick and mortar, back to much sowing and little reaping, back to making many bricks with too little straw, I carry with me yet a new and precious memory. In many a lonely hour yet to come I shall recall this visit here and remember that once more our loving mother put her kind hand upon my weary head and gave me her benediction. Oh mother of schools with half a century of grandeur behind you, grander in your calico than others in their velvet; walking with country shoes where satin slippers may not tread, richest of all schools, rich in faith, rich in love, rich in good works, rich in that strange spell, a name, and yet to be rich in silver and gold,—if ever I forget thee, may both my hands forget their cunning, and even a woman's tongue cleave to the roof of her mouth!

THE OLD AND THE NEW.

Mrs. M. L. SEVERANCE, Manchester, Vt.
(Emily A. Spencer, '58.)

In ages past, old chronicles relate,
A cavalcade passed out the Tabard gate;
A monk, a parson, prioress, and friar,
A knight, a clerk, a pardoner, and squire;
Full thirty souls, on pilgrimage intent,
Each pledged to tell a story as they went.

But, in the progress of this later day,
Hundreds of devotees are on their way;
Pilgrims alike, but in this motley crowd
No longer knight and friar are allowed,
But maidens, spinsters, madams manifold,
With parsons in the background; young and old
Equipped with satchel, bandbox, or umbrel—
Appendages in which the fair excel;
And each, less moderate than the band of old,
Has twenty stories waiting to be told.
If crowned saints can still be thought to know
The honors offered to their shrines below,
To gain the homage of such zealous crowd
A Becket would turn over in his shroud.

Ye drooping elms, upon whose front appears
The grace and beauty of your added years,
We reach our hands to you; no marks of age
Have marred the glory of your heritage;
The busy tread of generations gone
Who've sat beneath your shade and journeyed on,
Thinking their thoughts, going their varied ways,—
You keep no record of the bygone days;
You call no roll, you do not even sigh
As long processions yearly pass you by.
We name the names, within our hearts we hold
These trysting places of the days of old.
Ye mountains, and ye sunsets, tint and glow
That overspread the landscape then as now!
Ye all have journeyed with us, and have wrought
More than we know upon the roof of thought.

These classic halls we greet, though now no more
They echo to our footfalls as of yore;
Our pilgrim garb they may not recognize,
Nor read the story moistening in our eyes;
Truant, with half filled baskets we have come
Singing the praises of our early home.

Not the proud sovereign in her coronet,
On whose extended rule no sun has set,
Nor he who, by the Tiber, calmly waits
The willing tribute of unnumbered states,
Can summon a more loyal confidence,
Or gratitude more reverent and intense,
While vassals gather from two hemispheres
To weave the chaplet for their fifty years.

And ye instructors of the vanished past,
Your bread at morn upon the waters cast
We bring again to you; full oft since then
Has it brought nourishing to famished men,
And like the golden bough Proserpine
Requires of strangers who her realms would see,
Divided oft, the deftly horded store
Has still increased and multiplied the more.

And ye who patient at the helm hold sway
And bear the honors of a later day,
We scan your faces with expectant air,
Haply to find familiar features there.
Ah yes! We know you, there is magic now
To drive illusions from a fevered brow,
To know ye once were classmates; sisters, peers,
Our loved companions in the bygone years,
If ye've outstripped us running in life's race
Ye wear your honors with peculiar grace,
And in your gladness on this festal day
We lesser folk rejoice, as well we may.

As travelers in some antique aisle of prayer
Will note the battle flags suspended there,
And pause to murmur 'neath the somber yew,
This waved at Ivry, this at Waterloo,
So, too, our tattered banners placed on high
Tokens of conflict seem, and victory.
These hopeless rents, alas, what tales they tell
Of triumphs gained, or losses that befell!
They mark the ashes of extinguished fires,
Of aspirations, longings, dreams, desires;
They speak of struggle and temptation met,
Of folly, indecision, and regret,
Of beacon lights that, often faint and dim,
Led our repentant spirits back to Him
Whose blessings undeserved, day by day,
Spread their white tents at nightfall round our way.
The purposes we formed are unfulfilled;
The plans we cherished, and the hopes that thrilled
Like exhalations of the morning, rose
To mock us with their folly at its close.

Ye sought, O teachers of the long ago,
To give us fitting armor, and to show
That in the conflict waged with pride and pelf
The hero of the battle rules himself.
If by one hair's breadth you had failed in this
It had been easier our path to miss.

Ye who now learn the lesson we once learned,
And turn the pages that our fingers turned,
Youth, beauty, grace, a triple diadem
Ye wear, more lustrous than Brazilian gem;
Life's opening vistas greet your eager gaze,
Her phantoms lure you, and her siren's praise.
We glory in the privilege you share—
The opportunity to do and dare.
Fossils we seem to you, whose work is done,
Folded and laid away from air and sun.
But youth is patient, you will not forget
That in these fossils hearts are beating yet;
The cinders smolder in the silent urn,
But stir the embers and the fires will burn.
Between the greetings in an undertone
We listen for the voices we have known;
To us these halls seem echoing the tread
Of feet that move among the nameless dead.
A rustle as of wings is in the air,
And euthanasias whispered everywhere ;
The walls are frescoed with the wise, the good,
And all the place becomes a Holyrood.

We check the thought, the hour we would not dim
By selfish thought of saints or seraphim,
May we not hope that in yon happier sphere
Some thought is given to work accomplished here ?
As she whose loyal soul here prayed and wrought
To rear these walls will send a backward thought,
Will not some richer notes be made to ring
Because of gladness in the songs we sing ?
Perish the thought that souls can aught forget!
Beyond the stars they live and love us yet,
And if in heaven there be red-letter days
This one is crowned with most unusual praise.

The time, the place, to retrospect invite;
But if too long we strain with tear-dimmed sight
Our eyes into the past, we wrong the hour,
The present needs, the future's wondrous power.
Courage and consecration, hand in hand,
Have scattered blessings broadcast through the land,
The watchword of the past we make our own.
While all the fields lie yellow in the sun,

To-day is ours; who has a daring deed
To undertake, for life's most urgent need,
Must do it now; whoso would sing a song
Must strike the note at once, loud, clear, and strong.
Since first the flaming sword flashed high in air
And Eden closed upon a hapless pair,
No grander time the world has ever known,
No present richer than we call our own.
Oceans may bar and seas divide no more,
Highways of commerce stretch from shore to shore,
And no lone island in the tropic sea
Is foreign to our thought and sympathy;
The earth is wide, and, wander where you will,
Some load is there to lift, some void to fill.
" Go you where no one else will go," said she
Who sleeps beneath the ivy peacefully,—
"Do what none else will do, and then
Shall you bear healing to your fellow men."

A word to you whose armor waits your use,
You will allow, since age is garrulous.
Trust not in ease, the confidence you feel
Is in the temper of the untried steel;
Remember that the burnished surface glows
Only through friction which no respite knows.
If sitting at your *alma mater's* feet
You've talked with Æschylus in accents sweet,
Some soul from you a portion must have gained.
If you would keep the nectar you've obtained,
The world presents its murky atmosphere,
Its clouds for you to lift, its fog to clear.
Be not dismayed at what you find to do,
You need the world and it in turn needs you,
Its cares to lighten, and its loads to lift,
Its blame to suffer and its praise to sift.
These are the tasks that furnish golden keys
To open all your tenderest sympathies.
Where Nature smiles in grandeur and repose
Among the terrors of the Alpine snows,
Where bold Pilatus rears its cloud-capped rock
And frowns upon the heights of Bürgenstock,
And Rigi elevates its summit stern
Above the ancient city of Lucerne,
An old bridge hangs across the rapid Reuss,
Forming an angle, quaint and marvelous,
And antique pictures 'neath the rafters show
The Dance of Death to those that cross below.
—A sight to make one pause, and breathe a prayer
Before he treads the dusty thoroughfare.—
Arrow in hand the skeleton appears,
Marking his victims, in all climes and years,
The young, the gay, the aged, and the proud,
For each he has a winding sheet or shroud.

> But why at feast a skeleton intrude?
> Or why should jubilee a ghost include?
> Classmates and friends, death's arrows soon or late
> Will find us all, we may not hesitate.
> Could I but strike one ringing note to-day
> Which you, perchance, might hear, and bear away
> Into the heated tropics of your lives,
> When courage fails and only patience thrives,
> That note would be clear, steady, high:
> Be brave! be true! life's working moments fly.
> Morning is transient, dews and freshness cease,
> Noontide is crowded, evening brings release.
> Beyond the changing lights in which we dwell
> Eternal morning breaks, till then—farewell!

A solo, "One sweetly solemn thought," was sung by Miss Emily F. Paine, of '86.

The following message from the trustees, then in session, was received and read :—

The trustees of Mt. Holyoke Seminary cordially appreciate the work of the alumnæ in securing the Mary Lyon fund, and hereby express to the Association their thanks, and place this resolution on their records.

Miss ELLEN C. PARSONS, of '63, having been asked to speak upon "Sacred Hours at Mt. Holyoke," begun by saying that she would but touch upon "the sweet and suggestive theme," and she hoped others would follow with their reminiscences.

Miss Parsons said :—

I AM reminded of what geologists tell us. They say that in the wonderful economy of nature, minute crystals that once floated in the atmosphere and made the dying glory of past sunsets, lie now, dark and still, on the floor of the sea. So, too, of cosmic dust. It was once in the meteor. It flashed its way through space and left a trail of fire behind it, but now, cold and colorless, it lies with the relics of the sunset, down in the foundations of the deep.

Something like this I see in the imperishable, transmuted influence of peaceful, radiant hours, long ago sacred here and sacred to memory now. They were lifted into a rosy light of youthful hopes and ardors; they are laid away in our practical present. Below the heat and pressure and strain of our living to-day, lies buried their precious influence, wrought into the foundations of our Christian experience, and we recognize it there, whatever goes on at the surface.

Some of us since we went away from here have lived sheltered lives; later years were only an expansion of the peaceful ways we knew at South Hadley. But most of us the stress of life has carried away from our old moorings. It is only in the interludes that our ear catches an echo from the old halls in the valley behind the mountains. But we do hear it. In the busy haunts of men, I have heard again Miss Hopkins's voice. In the clatter of Broadway, I have gone again to prayer-meeting and sat beside a classmate who has been in heaven these many summers.

Let me remind you of the hymns which are a prominent association of those sacred hours. Confidently we sung,—

"How firm a foundation"!

With what daring we repeated it,—

"Never, no never, no never forsake"!

Time has tested us, and I long ago gave up singing some lines that never staggered me then. It may be that some others, with me, have grown dumb before this,—

"The changes that will surely come I do not fear to see."

One used to wail like the night wind through the dining-hall. How old, how fairly tottering with the weight of years, we used to feel singing,—

"A few more storms shall beat
On this wild, rocky shore."

Another is forever associated with Miss Fiske's voice and the excitement of moving day,—

"Calm me, my God, and keep me calm."—

While·

"Depth of mercy!—can there be
Mercy still reserved for me?"

belonged to Fast Day,

"Everlasting arms of love,"

was for recess meeting, a sweet pillow to go to sleep on.

I will not enlarge upon the recollections we all share of the marching hymns we sung in the morning,—

"Awake, my soul, stretch every nerve,"

when we had hard lessons before us, and the hymns of victory such as Mrs. Gulliver gave us in Bible class once, with a peculiar triumph in her tone,—

"Oh where are kings and empires now
Of old that went and came?
But, Lord, thy Church is praying yet,
A thousand years the same!"

The hymns were an element of those hours that we easily lay hold of in a retrospect. We readily recall, too, some definite instruction from the desk. All of us have passages indelibly stamped upon our memories, as applied by different leaders of our services. Such a passage to me is that of one who "drew a bow at a venture and smote the king of Israel between the joints of the harness;" and I have only to hear that text to recall dear Miss Hopkins in her bright morning-gown, her pale, earnest face and the delicate irony of her tone as she repeated now and again "drew a bow *at a venture*." Hannah's prayer was fixed by Miss Fiske's illuminating; so, too, what I thank her for to-day, a cheerful, happy way of taking Sunday. "If one pie was better than another," she said, "I would have that on Sunday. I would exalt it as a day of privilege."

Prof. Park, in one of his famous sermons on a Fast Day, painted a certain passage in unfading colors. It was this: "And they were in the way going up to Jerusalem; and Jesus went before them." I never since could read that verse without seeing our Saviour's majestic march in advance of his disciples, up toward Gethsemane and Calvary, glowing with divine resolve to drain the cup his Father gave him.

It were easy to multiply instances, but others will mention them. It was a great amount of religious instruction we had here, and the most of it cannot be gathered up in quotations. It did for us what the sun does in bleaching the cloth. Like the sunset dust in the ocean sediment, it has gone into the warp and woof of our lives, into our thinking and purposes.

With regard to the character of that teaching, as a whole, it was not sentimental. As a friend was saying to me, "They did not prophesy to us smooth things." In my time, at least, it was what we could understand and assimilate. It was practical. The awfulness of standing around this world idle, while life is flying, Christ's kingdom coming, that was a prominent feature of it. Self-denial, "we are not our own,"—you will bear me witness, *that* vein was mined very often.

When Dr. Kirk came, our pride and self-will got tremendous blows, dealt with Elijah-like hand. From Amherst they used to bring over great thoughts of God's providence and grace, and Dr. Tyler's sermon about "pitching the tent towards Sodom," and Dr. Seelye's upon "When the commandment came, sin revived and I died," were nails driven in a sure place. Nor, in passing, would I omit to mention the very considerable influence of the preaching of Mr. Mead, afterwards Prof. Mead, of Oberlin. I regret that I cannot recall a single sermon of his, but hundreds will say, as I do, that the stimulating character and elevated tone of his pulpit were one of the privileges of our period.

If there was any lack in the body of religious instruction that we received at this seminary,—and I hesitate to intimate any deficiency, but I know we have not come here simply for the purpose of adulation,— I should say the loving kindness of our Heavenly Father was less emphasized than is right. Our "God who giveth us all things richly to enjoy" was not held up to us so often as to produce the strongest impression. My recollection is of looking through the fence of the commandments and being oftener led into the wilderness with John the Baptist than to the wedding feast with Jesus.

As to the prayer-meetings, how many there were to make their impression! They may have been something overdone and have suffered from constraint upon attendance; but there's nothing perfect here, and many unspeakably precious hours we had in them. They were guarding influences; they hallowed our friendships. One of the most important results of those recess meetings, as it seems to me, is the training they afforded for the service of prayer in the Church of God. Many of us have been able to come to the rescue of a woman's prayer-meeting, or a missionary meeting or Sabbath-school service where there was no one to pray,—not because we were any more fit for that service than others were, but simply because we were in the habit of hearing our voices and could command them. The young people's prayer-meetings, so common now, and Christian Endeavor Societies, are giving this training as it was not formerly given.

You will expect allusions to the "half-hour" and to Fast Day. I know there are many here who made a richer use of these sacred hours than I, and whose experience, if they would tell it, would be worth our coming together to hear. I only give a common and perhaps below the average experience. Whatever we regret in our lives it is not these things. We are glad for the steady, recurring opportunity of the one, and the special opportunity of the other. I suppose we all remember the awesomeness of our first Fast Day. It was like the shadow of Sinai. We heard thunderings and a voice that shook the earth. Each year softened the first impression, but those days stand out, yet, in Doré outlines. I remember a meeting in room A, at the breakfast bell, on such a day, with special joy. Perhaps it was the entire voluntariness of it, in a January morning when we might have slept over, in a not very warm, neither very light, recitation-room. But, as I recall those bright congenial spirits, and the solemn sincerity with which we began that day with God and weighed eternal interests, that bare room seems a place to take off my shoes.

It is a good thing for a house to have foundations, but it isn't the way for a man to live in his cellar. It is a very poor thing we are making of life if we are trusting to sacred influences of the past, to our Mt. Holyoke training decades ago. It is not what God did for us once, but what we are permitting him to do now, that we are to look to. And isn't it dishonoring our Heavenly Father to think for a moment that he could bless us any more in the past, or here, than he can bless us now, or anywhere he puts us? No hallowed hours set round with leisure, then, were better for us than that last prayer snatched from between the upper and nether millstones of a day of care. We were not any better Christians when we sung so lightly, "never, no never," than when beside the death-bed of the beloved, we struggled with the thought, Has he forsaken? When I think of those days of fasting kept by regulation, which we deliberately set ourselves to observe, and compare them with those days of humiliation and fasting and prayer which we have had to keep since, whether we would or not, when God has sent us to our knees,—*those* are to *these* as the knight who goes out gayly to find a combatant at the tournament, to the soldier who goes to real war.

But it seems to me the chief thing we have to say to each other on this memorable occasion is, that God is *for* us always. He is for us now just as much as in those old days when we sucked instruction from the breasts of *alma mater;* when we ate honey out of the honey-comb. God has beset us "behind" in privileges. He has also beset us "before" with his appointments, and we may feel his "hand" upon us in blessing.

Blessed the memory of all those who taught us of Him! Peace on them that helped us! Peace, forever, on all that prayed with us and for us!

HYMN.

MRS. DR. GAMWELL, WESTFIELD.
(Sarah DeWolf, '61.)

O, THOU, in whose sight, like a tale that is told,
The centuries pass, and the nations grow old!
From shore unto shore, and from sea unto sea,
Who builds for Eternity buildeth for Thee.

Consecrated the life that this temple did raise,
Consecrated to Thee! O, Thou Ancient of Days!
Thou wert her Defender, in darkness and light,
Her Refuge by day, and her Song in the night.

Though the years that have passed are rolled up like a scroll,
She built for the ages, she built for the soul;
'Mid the hills round about, on this flower-covered sod,
We stand where she stood, and we praise Thee, O God.

O, Thou, in whose sight, like a tale that is told,
The centuries pass, and the nations grow old!
From age unto age, and from sea unto sea,
Who builds for Eternity buildeth for Thee!

On being called upon to lead in prayer, Mrs. Rhea (Sarah J. Foster of '55) said :—

MY dear friends, I want to see your faces. When one has been a missionary for ten years and looked upon the faces of heathen women, she has a great desire to look upon the faces of Christian women. There is an unspeakable fascination in the beauty of a Christian woman's face, a cultivated, educated, Christian woman's face. And when I look upon your faces and think of those dark faces I have looked upon, there comes upon me an unutterable longing for that beauty. But the light that shines on your faces is but the reflection of heaven's light.

I am glad of that mute appeal that hangs before us. [A map of the world.] O that Christian women may be reminded of those women on whom this light has never fallen! These days are like a foretaste of heaven. I have had a new definition of heaven since coming here: it seems to me that it is the infinite love of God flowing unrestricted through finite hearts. I do not believe there is anything here to restrict that love. If there is any one here who feels alone, then we will concentrate on that lonely heart the love of Mt. Holyoke and set it on fire. It seems to me there is love enough here to flood the world.

After prayer, the following paper was read by Mrs. Moses Smith:—

THE FUTURE OF MT. HOLYOKE SEMINARY.

It requires no gift of sibyl or pythoness to see that Mt. Holyoke Seminary stands to-day in the presence of an outlook of great opportunity and signal power. Its founding and its history are prophetic of its future. The standard lifted up by Mary Lyon, bearing the inspired words, "That our daughters may be as corner-stones, polished after the similitude of a palace," has been borne across our continent, planted in the land of the Alhambra, amid the darkness of Africa, and beneath the shadows of Himalayas and the Taurus. The half century that spans the life of our *alma mater* has no peer in the great number of energizing, startling forces which have entered the world. The stream of history has been turned from its wonted channels, human life and thought have been revolutionized. In the complexity of energies we catch a glimpse of the meaning of Ezekiel's vision of the wheels within wheels bearing on the Messiah's throne. Antagonistic forces long dormant are aroused to battle; the earth is shaken by the conflict; faint hearts quake and send up signals of alarm; yet out of what seems to us chaos, God's ruling hand brings most beneficent results. It is easy to see that scientific discoveries and inventions have given men a kingly mastery over the material world, making matter the medium of thought, and truth ministrant to mental and spiritual life. Our dainty little friend, steam, with a puff and a clatter of cogs, sends forth myriads of sibylline leaves, touching life in the "heavens and the earth and the waters under the earth," or with trains of commerce in its wake thunders across the continent, leaping gorges and piercing mountains in its eagerness to keep pace with the thought and life of man. The domestication of the wild flame of the clouds to be our most gentle servant, to bear our messages, to carry the tones of our voices over leagues of land, has alone revolutionized the world. Time and space annihilated, the ends of the earth stand face to face. The length of a continent is no more than the width of the highway between Jerusalem and Jericho, across which we hear the cry of the wounded, compelling us to choose whether we will pass by on the other side.

That prophecy of the Revelation, "There shall be no more sea," which was to be the sign manual of the "new heavens and the new earth," is practically fulfilled. To-day the Atlantic is only two seconds wide. All are conscious of the giant strides the world has taken under the action of these forces, and the most casual observer sees how they project themselves on the horizon of the future. Other energies, less evident in their methods, but more far reaching in their results, have wrought revolutions in the relations of man to man. Witness the conquest of democratic principles and the resultant changes in the relation of rulers and subjects; the assertions of the spirit of liberty for the unshackling of millions.

The point that most interests us and which is most pertinent to the occasion is the radical change which fifty years have wrought in the place and power of woman. In this result Mt. Holyoke Seminary has been a potent factor, doubtless working better than she knew.

Mt. Holyoke Seminary, unique in its plan and purpose, the first embodiment of the thought of collegiate education for woman, has from the outset been a revolutionizing force in society. Working in silent strength, this institution has not always been evident among the more noisy forces that have literally "come hither to turn the world upside down." It is within my memory that a woman who aspired to authorship was supposed to do so at the expense of all truly feminine pursuits, and writers in the columns of an organ of no less dignity than the New York *Tribune* of that date urged that arithmetic was a useless study for a girl and would only tend to make her masculine. What possible use could a girl have for a knowledge of arithmetic? Not much, indeed, if such as they could have stayed the hand of Providence. But God's hand is never stayed from purposes of good to the human race, and he was preparing for himself a mighty force in the uplifting of the nations.

Home is, and ever will be, woman's primal kingdom. This is in the nature of things. Tender ministries to little children are more angelic service than anything else on earth. It is trite in this presence to say that the mother whose horizon has been broadened by culture, so that she is interested to watch the great developments in science, in politics, in theology, will assuredly lay firm foundations of character in her children and lead them forth with aspirations to high endeavor. The world has learned that woman is none the less queen in the home because she has taken her degree at college and may, if she so elect, enter the medical profession, plead at the bar, speak from the pulpit or platform. Woman is never to do man's work, but God is leading her on to heights where she sees something of the wide fields meant for her tilling. Be not alarmed, conservative soul, where God wants woman there he will place her, and neither you nor I can prevent it.

We who, a generation ago, were taught such delicacies of propriety as that the masculine ear might not listen to the feminine voice asking for a blessing on our food, have sometimes asked ourselves if we had unconsciously stepped into a new world, with a new order of life, when we found ourselves kneeling in prayer by the wounded soldier, while men and officers reverently bowed the head, as much in reverence to womanhood as to the act of worship; or, in later days, standing before audiences of men and women too intent on the great themes of reformation and salvation to ask whether the voice that moved them to endeavor was that of man or woman. In the presence of the great questions that command the attention of the world to-day, that question is trivial. We did not forget the instructions of our honored teachers, and we gratefully record that we garnered then treasures of strength and power for life's work which have not failed us in time of need. But on this point of what it is fitting for a woman to do the teachings of the past were not adapted to the exigencies in which we afterward found ourselves, and we had to leave them with the things that were, while we pressed on to those before.

For any adequate understanding of the trend of the world, we must remember that man is the pivotal point of creation and history. Man is himself the reason for all things that be. Sin and salvation are the problems which the ages are solving, and woman is the prime factor in the solution. Not long since, in a company of intelligent, widely read ladies and gentlemen, the question was asked, What fact of the present century is fraught with the greatest power for the uplifting of the human race? The French revolution, the aggressions of the British empire, the application of steam as a motor, the discovery and application of the principles that govern the use of electricity, were named, before a lady ventured to say, "The higher education of woman and her resultant power, especially as a teacher of Christianity." For a moment all were silent, dumb with amazement at the presumption of the reply; when they were reminded that Christianity is to-day the dominant force of the world, that mothers and homes are the centers of power, and that woman is the chief agent by which the leaven of the gospel is hidden in those centers, the answer was convincing.

God in his providence has brought woman into personal contact with the forces that are moving the world. She has learned that her responsibilities may not be delegated to husband or sons. She has felt that inspiration that is begotten only of the consciousness that she lives in a day when her life cannot be so retired that she may not if she will touch the springs of action that shall compass the earth. There is the promise of great power in this broadening sphere of woman's life. The imprint of God's law of action, "progress," is upon the world; progress sometimes of the tidal wave, more often of the unfolding bud, but always onward. The world of to-day is a different world from that on which Mary Lyon looked even with her far-seeing eye. Look along whatever line you will, not only is the external life changed, but the very methods of thought are new. All business, from that of the bootblack to the millionaire, has now to be conducted by some methods adapted to the quickened urgency of the times. Old methods and old machinery must be cast aside, and new ones with greater power and broader scope must be installed. The same general principles that govern a successful business enterprise of the day are needed and used by our institutions of learning.

It behooves the present conservators of this seminary to cause the institution to be organized and equipped in a manner befitting the possibilities of its promised powers. The first need that it may fittingly meet the demands of the future is ample endowment. The means by which it could do its God-given work in the last half century are not adequate to the changed condition of the world to-day. As well expect to conduct the present business of the world by the methods of a century ago as to expect the seminary without endowment to realize the grand possibilities of the future. There is money enough; a wise and well directed effort will secure needed endowments.

Along with the endowment there should be such an enlarging and re-arranging of the course of study as shall entitle the institution to the name of college and place it where Mary Lyon placed it—the leading woman's college in the land. With the estimate of woman and woman's place in the world which prevailed when Mary Lyon founded this school of learning, the name seminary was the nearest approach to college that would be tolerated. To have proposed to found a woman's college would have roused grave fears and brought opprobrium on the enterprise. But the world has taken giant strides onward since that day, and the wise men and women of to-day who found institutions adapt the courses of study and the name to the new understanding of woman's place and the present need of the world for her service.

Names, like people, live their generation, do their work, and are "gathered unto their fathers"; may they also await a resurrection day! This school might far excel some of the present colleges in its classical and scientific instruction, yet without the name which to-day signifies that such work is done, that argus-eyed censor, public opinion, would relegate it to a secondary position. There are weighty reasons why Mt. Holyoke should have every equipment of endowment, of building, of apparatus, of instructors, needed to place it and keep it in the first rank of colleges.

The most distinguishing feature in the history of this school has been its religious power. It has had a "Christian renown." How our hearts burn within us as we remember the solemn fasts, and the glory of the conscious presence of the Holy Ghost! The germinal, vital faith of the founder met the promised response from God, and year after year he has set the seal of his presence on the souls of the pupils, and they have gone forth to make radiant centers of Christian power the world over. For the honor of God, a correspondingly high standard, a broad intellectual and æsthetic culture should be maintained, that the highest possibility of well-balanced womanhood may here be realized.

In this connection I beg to be allowed to make one proposition, or rather to utter a cherished hope. In that time which I trust is in the near future, when endowments shall have been secured and a larger order of things adopted, let this institution have a department of Biblical instruction. I gratefully recognize the prominence always given to the study of the Bible, and also the arrangement by which every member of the household has time for both social and private prayer. These have been the channels of God's wondrous presence and power; may they remain forever! But there are reasons to-day why women should not only be familiar with the truths of Biblical revelation, but should be trained in exegesis and in methods of imparting spiritual truths to ignorant minds. Christianity is the dominant power of the world to-day. I speak not boastfully but with a reverent sense of the responsibility when I say that Christian woman holds a power over the eternal destinies of the race never before wielded by human hands—the power to hide the leaven of the gospel in the hearts of the millions of mothers who may never hear the angels' song, "Unto thee this day a Saviour is born," except from the lips of a Christian woman. Young men who are to be teachers of Christianity are fitted, or unfitted, for their work by a three years' course in a theological seminary. To-day young women are going forth, by scores and fifties and hundreds, to be teachers of Christianity, with far too little preparation for their work. This cannot long continue. There are already plans maturing for the establishment of a school for the training of women for this wide field. Why should not Mt. Holyoke College have an endowed chair for that department? It would be in harmony with the history and spirit of this institution.

In the most brilliant part of our winter evening sky, where Orion and the Pleiades rule in beauty, there is one star more beautiful than any other. The wise men of Arabia appointed it to lead the zodiac and called its name Aldebaran, "the one that leads the way." In the precession of the equinoxes, Aries has come to the front and now marshals the celestial hosts. But that star in the eye of Taurus still shines with unequaled beauty and men still call it Aldebaran, "the leading one." Among the constellations of woman's colleges that meet our present vision, and among those that are yet to climb higher in the sky of our horizon, Mt. Holyoke is the Aldebaran, the one that leads the way. Another like Aries may come to the front; but, if the conservators of this institution are equal to their opportunities, the world shall ever point to the clear, brilliant light of Mt. Holyoke Seminary, the star of chiefest honor, the Aldebaran.

The following resolutions were then presented by Mrs. Smith, Miss Brigham being in the chair:—

Resolved—That the alumnæ of Mt. Holyoke Seminary, assembled on this auspicious occasion, hereby gratefully record their high appreciation of the large results secured by the honored board of trustees in new and improved buildings, valuable apparatus, and other costly appliances adapted to the needs of a growing institution.

Resolved—That we note with genuine satisfaction and pride the enlargement of the course of study and the steady maintenance on the part of the faculty of the Christian aim and scholarship for which this institution has merited world-wide honor.

Resolved—That the interests of higher education to-day as well as the aim of the illustrious founder of this institution demand without delay that an ample endowment should be provided.

Resolved—That we believe the time has fully come when this seminary should itself take the name Mt. Holyoke College, and also establish a curriculum befitting the name.

Action was taken on the resolutions separately. The first and second were adopted without debate. With reference to the third the question was raised whether it would not be better to work for one department rather than for a general endowment; but the conviction was expressed that the institution should lead in all departments, and should be so amply endowed that it can be furnished with the best advantages to be had. The promise "Open thy mouth wide and I will fill it" was quoted, and the resolution was adopted without change. It was moved to amend the fourth by substituting "Mary Lyon University" for "Mt. Holyoke College." In view of two considerations the amendment was lost. One was the reminder by Miss Edwards that the college curriculum proposed had not yet been adopted, and as the institution had not even become a college, it could hardly take the name university. The other was the well-known wish of the founder, "You must not call this Mary Lyon's school. I regard it so truly a child of Providence that I do not like to have my name made prominent." The latter objection held likewise against the other names proposed—"Mary Lyon College and Mt. Holyoke Seminary" and "Mary Lyon College." But all agreed in desiring a full college course, without abandoning the present one, and the resolution as adopted read as follows:—

Resolved—That we believe the time has fully come when this seminary shall become a college having a seminary department associated with it similar to the course of study which has been so successful for fifty years.

Adjourned.

SEMI-CENTENNIAL EXERCISES.

THURSDAY, JUNE 23.

THE exercises on Thursday morning were held in a large tent. President Seelye of Amherst College presided. After the anthem, " We will rejoice and be glad," by the seminary choir, Rev. Dr. Laurie offered the following invocation :—

O Lord, our Saviour and our Redemer, we come together at Thy call. We claim Thy promise,—" where two or three are gathered together in my name, there am I." We pray that the rain which Thou art sending to refresh the earth may only show forth more gloriously Thy power to bless us while we are together. Direct Thou in every truth that may be uttered, in every impression that may be received, and may Thy name be glorified in all, for Thy name's sake. Amen.

The choir then sang the anthem " Sing to Jehovah."

HISTORICAL ADDRESS,

BY THE PRESIDENT OF THE BOARD OF TRUSTEES,

REV. WM. S. TYLER, D.D., LL. D., OF AMHERST COLLEGE.

Mr. President, Trustees, Alumnæ, Teachers and Pupils of Mt. Holyoke Seminary. Ladies and Gentlemen:—

AN institution at its semi-centennial is young. A college professor is old at the fiftieth anniversary of his professorship. That a professor who last year celebrated his fiftieth anniversary should be the chief speaker at the semi-centennial celebration of an institution this year is a manifest incongruity,—an incongruity, however, for which *he* is not responsible. If the trustees had duly considered the fitness of things, they would have chosen for their orator on this occasion, not the oldest, but the youngest of their own number, or perchance some college tutor instead of a veteran professor, or, better still perhaps, some juvenile pastor, the pet of his parish, especially of the young ladies of his flock, or, at any rate, one of the youngest of the fifty eloquent orators who have graced an equal number of our Mt. Holyoke anniversaries. Even the ancient and venerable university which lately celebrated the two hundred and fiftieth anniversary of its founding is so young in comparison with the universities of the Old World that the accomplished orator of the day felt under the necessity of apologizing for the celebration of so brief an existence. How then can Holyoke, with less than one-fifth of Harvard's years,—young and blushing, scarcely yet in her teens,—how can Holyoke hold up her head and celebrate to-day!

There is, however, this justification of such celebrations in our age and country: events now and here succeed each other with such amazing rapidity that the work of a thousand years is often accomplished in half a century, and modern science has invested men with prerogatives approaching those of Him with whom a thousand years are as one day, and one day as a thousand years.

Besides, we do not celebrate ourselves on an occasion like this. We come together to revisit the old homestead, to rekindle the sacred fire on the altar of our hearts, and, while we take each other by the hand and renew our acquaintance with one another, to revive the memories of our fathers and mothers, to contemplate the wisdom and the virtues of the men and women of a former generation, and to learn the lessons taught us in their lives.

It is difficult for the young ladies who hear me to imagine, and not easy for the oldest of my audience to realize, what the condition of the country and the people was at the time when Mt. Holyoke Seminary first opened its doors to receive pupils; how great the changes are which have taken place in our territory, population, society, government, education, and religion during the last fifty years. Fifty years ago Texas, New Mexico, and California belonged to Mexico; Oregon and Washington Territory were in fierce dispute between the United States and Great Britain; and Alaska, which stretches as far west of San Francisco as Maine extends east of that city, was a part of the vast empire of the Czar. In 1835 there were not five thousand white inhabitants between Lake Michigan and the Pacific Ocean. In 1840 the population of Chicago was 4,500; it now exceeds 700,000. In 1834 the city of Milwaukee consisted of two log houses; now it has a population of 125,000. In 1830 New York city boasted of 200,000 inhabitants; according to the census of 1880, it then had a million and a quarter, and two millions and a quarter within a distance of eight miles from the city hall. Within the last half-century, the population of the United States has increased from fifteen millions to sixty millions; and the country has grown in wealth, in agriculture, manufactures, and commerce, in the value of real estate and personal property, in mines and canals and railroads; and the people have advanced in the conveniences, luxuries, and elegancies of life, in fine houses and beautiful grounds and style of living, in the use and display of gold and silver and precious stones, more than in population. And, what is still more suggestive of prudent and patriotic forethought and anxiety, the cities have grown in population and wealth at the expense of the country. The valleys of the East and the prairies of the West have been enriched by drawing on the resources of the hill towns of

New England and the Middle States. Fifty years ago only one-fifteenth of our people lived in cities of over 12,000 inhabitants, now one-fourth of our entire population live in such cities. During the last half-century wealth and population have been running down from the hill towns of New England into the manufacturing villages and the great cities, and flowing out all over the greater West, as rapidly and irresistibly as the streams that take their rise in these hills flow into the ocean.

Nor can we forget on this occasion that Amherst College and Mt. Holyoke Seminary and the American Board of Foreign Missions owe their very existence to those hill towns in which Mary Lyon and Levi Parsons and Pliny Fiske and Jonas King were born, and Samuel J. Mills and his associates prayed, and Deacon Avery and Colonel Rice tilled and tithed, nay, ten times tithed their poor, rough farms, and Theophilus Packard and Edward Hitchcock preached, and the Franklin County Association planned for the education of pastors and teachers in coming generations. Nor should our great cities and our greater West forget that they owe to these hill towns a debt of gratitude and service which all their wealth and their largest liberality can never pay.

In 1837 the gold of Australia and the gold and silver of California were still undiscovered. There was then no Panama railroad, no canal across the Isthmus of Suez. Travel and commerce passed from the Atlantic to the Pacific coast only in sailing vessels around Cape Horn or the Cape of Good Hope. An iron track across the continent was an enterprise too bold for the imagination to conceive. A voyage by steam-ship across the Atlantic men of science had demonstrated to be a physical impossibility, since no ship could carry fuel enough to propel it over so vast a distance and for so long a time. To come nearer home, there was a railroad from Boston to Worcester; its extension over the mountains to Albany was contemplated as a daring and doubtful undertaking. A railroad from Springfield to New York was in the still more distant future. The stage-coach was almost the only public conveyance by which the teachers and pupils of Holyoke Seminary came from and returned to their *distant* homes in New England and New York! Let the young ladies of the present day think of this when they are *tempted* to grumble at their inconveniences (that they actually *grumble* or fret is of course not to be supposed), and let them be thankful that they can now go a thousand miles in less time and with fewer hardships than in 1837 their predecessors could go a hundred.

But what touches the heart of a school girl away from home even more tenderly than inconveniences of travel was the expense of postage. The tariff for the conveyance of any single-sheet letter, however light or heavy, over one hundred miles, was eighteen and three-fourths cents; over four hundred miles, twenty-five cents; and for every sheet or scrap of paper added to a single sheet, double postage. Billet-doux were costly affairs then; if written daily they counted up fast. It should be added, however, that the young ladies did not have the worst of it, for custom made it the duty, and of course gallantry made it the privilege and the pleasure of the young gentlemen to pay the postage at both ends. Furthermore, both sexes wrote less frequently, and avenged themselves on an absurd law by writing on very generous, sometimes on what were called "mammoth," sheets.

The day of Queen Anne houses and lawn mowers, pictures and decorations, bric-a-brac and jewelry had not yet dawned. The first generation of Mt. Holyoke teachers and pupils rarely wore gold, jewels, or pearls. Mr. Buckingham, the English traveler who visited the country in those days, was struck with the comparative infrequency with which American ladies wore diamonds even in fashionable parties in New York city. Travelers nowadays see with surprise American ladies wear diamonds at their own breakfast tables. And if we may believe newspapers and novels (not the best authority it is true), some American ladies of the present day not only flaunt their diamonds on every occasion at home, but crowd ocean steamers in the same flashy attire, astonish London and Paris by their gold and jewels, dazzle the watering places and summer resorts of England and the Continent by their brilliancy, and captivate the aristocracy of Europe by their charms. I venture to predict, however, that among such American women no graduate of Mt. Holyoke Seminary will be found, probably no graduate of any of the schools and colleges that are counted among the daughters of Holyoke.

The widest and deepest chasm that has opened between 1837 and 1887 is the great civil war which cost us thousands of millions of money and half a million of lives, and was worth all it cost; which not only abolished slavery, but perpetuated the Union, strengthened the Constitution, created the Nation, changed the whole policy of the government, opened the way for the emancipation and education not only of the slaves but of the white population of the South, inspired the people of the whole country with a new enthusiasm for union, liberty, justice, and humanity, and placed the United States in the very forefront of the great nations of the world in prestige, in power, in moral and political influence.

But, incredible and almost inconceivable as the changes are which have taken place during the last half-century, it is not less difficult for us, in these days of woman's colleges and enlargement of woman's sphere in every direction, to conceive of the opposition which Mary Lyon had to encounter and the obstacles she had to surmount in the founding of Mt. Holyoke Seminary. In Northampton, where Smith College, with an endowment and curriculum equal to those of colleges for the other sex, is now educating three hundred girls, and where girls now enjoy the same advantages in all the public schools, including the high school, as boys, and get as good an education as boys, if not better on an average, it was voted in town meeting in 1788, "not to be at any expense for schooling girls"; and girls were not allowed to *attend* the public schools until 1792, and then only after a hard struggle. In Hatfield, where the founder of Smith College was born and buried, the only school privilege which girls enjoyed, less than a century ago, was that of sitting on the doorstep of the school-house in the summer time and hearing the boys read and recite their lessons, and very few enjoyed even this poor privilege of *looking* into the earthly paradise. Less than a century ago the laws of Massachusetts did not recognize woman as a teacher in the public schools. In 1837 there were 2,370 men and 3,591 women teachers in Massachusetts; in 1886 there were 1,060 men and 8,610 women teachers. In 1837 the average compensation of female teachers in Massachusetts was $5.38 a month (with "board around"—which was in fact working their passage and doing missionary, perhaps housekeeping, service as they went); now it is $43.85 a month. Mary Lyon received seventy cents a week and her board for her first services as a teacher at Shelburne Falls. Susannah Whitney, a veteran teacher, who, after teaching fifty years in the public schools of Boston and the vicinity, has just resigned her position, had a salary of $25 a year when she began her work in 1836. In looking about for a place in the West for the location of a school for girls, Miss Grant (later known as Mrs. Banister) records that she had seen or heard of only one place in all Ohio off the Reserve, where teaching took anything like its proper rank, and says that she heard a lady of intelligence, refinement, and Christian character say of a young woman who left her home to engage in teaching: "That is a great coming down for her, for she was a great belle." Xenophon in his Memorabilia implies that parents in ancient Greece thought it their duty "to educate their sons and to *protect* their daughters." Half a century ago American parents had scarcely advanced beyond this idea. Of course girls in the better families were taught at home, to read and write and sew and embroider; and in many cases, like that of the wife of John Adams, this home education bore the richest and choicest fruit. There were also private schools more or less numerous and of various degrees of good or evil influence, although they were always expensive and usually superficial, cultivating the manners with little or no mental discipline or moral and religious culture, and preparing young women for a life of fashion and frivolity rather than for duty and service in the family, in the church, and in the world.

A few choice spirits, pioneers in the higher education of women, were laboring hard, and not without some partial success, to create a better public sentiment, to introduce a new era—the era of schools for young women, in which sound learning should be united with pure and earnest evangelical religion. There was Mrs. Emma Hart Willard, the brilliant and accomplished teacher, author of original and popular textbooks and founder of the Troy Female Seminary, who devoted her life to the education and elevation of her sex, who conceived a plan for *Improving Female Education* which was so high and broad and deep that she felt it required endowments and facilities which could be furnished only by the patronage of the State. Accordingly she pressed it upon the consideration of the legislature of New York with all her own power of personal persuasion and seconded by the personal and political influence of Governor Clinton, who urged the legislature "not to be deterred by common-place ridicule from extending their munificence to this meritorious institution." But, failing to secure a legislative appropriation, she went on her own solitary and sublime way and built up the private school which has ever since been associated with her name, which prospered greatly, and sent out well trained teachers and well educated, refined ladies in great numbers into every state of the Union, so long as the founders, Mrs. Willard and her son, were at the head, and then, like other private schools without endowments, became extinct.

There was Rev. Joseph Emerson, the Christian scholar and gentleman whom all his pupils revered as a father, the patriarch of normal teachers when as yet there were no normal schools, who showed his respect for women by teaching and treating them as the gentler but not the weaker, the other but not the inferior, sex, and, in proof of that position, had only to point to Zilpah P. Grant and Mary Lyon, and many others in his school less known but not less thoroughly educated and fitted for the work of life. His pupils, widely scattered over the land as teachers and as wives and mothers, accomplished much for the education and elevation of their sex; but his school, as if it were built on wheels, migrated from Byfield to Saugus and from Saugus to Wethersfield, and ceased to move only when, with the failing health of its founder, it ceased to live.

There was Miss Grant, afterwards Mrs. Banister, whose biography has been well written in that little volume of the American Tract Society under the appropriate title, "The Use of a Life," and the poetry and romance of whose life I hope you have all read in Gail Hamilton's spicy article, entitled "An American Queen," published a year ago in the *North American Review*, though I hope you did not accept the writer's arbitrary but characteristic assumption that her religious experience was all "hocus-pocus and abracadabra." With Miss Lyon as her assistant, Miss Grant made her school at Derry so prosperous and so powerful in moulding the characters and shaping the lives as well as forming the minds of her pupils, that her board of liberal (?) trustees became jealous of her evangelical influence, and showed their liberality by trying to dictate what her teaching and influence should be. Too conscientious, too self-respecting, and too Christian to submit to this, taking all her teachers and the most and best of her pupils with her, she removed her school to Ipswich—a place which to this day is best known to the general public as the site of that school—a school which, if it had been organized and endowed and thus perpetuated according to the idea which Miss Grant and Miss Lyon cherished and sought to realize together, but which Miss Lyon had to execute alone, might perhaps have been the Mt. Holyoke of that generation and the Wellesley College of the present day.*

Those were able teachers, those were excellent schools. But they wanted endowment, organization, and public recognition. They needed

---

*Of course there were other teachers and other schools that would deserve mention in a complete history of the pioneers in the higher education of woman, such as Bradford Academy, Miss Beecher's School in Hartford, Albany Female Academy, Ontario Female Seminary, Pittsfield Young Ladies' Institute, Elmira College, etc. But no attempt is here made at completeness. Only illustrative specimens are given and particularly those of which Holyoke was, as it were, in the line of succession.

a curriculum, a stadium, and a goal; in other words, they needed a fixed course of study, permanent boards of management and instruction, and established conditions of graduation; and of course they failed of stability, permanence, perpetuity. In short, they wanted just what academies, colleges, and universities for young men had enjoyed from time immemorial, but what was deemed unnecessary in the education of young women.

But the objections to this idea of equalizing the educational advantages of the two sexes were many and various, and not always consistent with each other, or consonant with the courtesy due to the gentler sex. It was an innovation uncalled for, unheard of until now since the foundation of the world, and unthought of now except by a few strong-minded women and radical men who would level all distinctions, and overturn the foundations of the family, of society, of the church, and of the state. It was unnatural, unphilosophical, unscriptural, unpractical and impracticable, unfeminine and antichristian; in short, all the epithets in the dictionary that begin with *un*, *in*, or *anti* were hurled against it and heaped upon it. Had not Paul said: "I suffer not a woman to teach, nor to usurp authority over the man, but to be in silence. And if they will learn anything, let them ask their husbands at home." It would be the entering wedge to women's preaching, practicing, lecturing, voting, ruling, buying and selling, doing everything that men do, and perhaps doing it better than men do, and so overstocking all the trades and professions. *Hinc illæ lacrymæ!* hence, in part at least, these tears. At the same time it was insisted that such occupations as these and such studies as mathematics and philosophy were not suited to the tastes or the capacities of women; they didn't want them and wouldn't undertake them; and if they did, such studies would ruin their health, impair their gentleness, delicacy, modesty, and refinement, unsex them and unfit them for their proper sphere. In short, it was like the famous logico-illogical borrowed kettle: 1. It was never borrowed; 2. It had been returned; 3. It was broken when it was borrowed; 4. It was whole when it was returned.

Miss Lyon herself did not escape severe criticism. Her pupils and associates loved and admired her. All who knew her honored her. But it was not then the fashion to praise her. She had not yet been canonized. She was well nigh a martyr, but she was not yet a saint. She was herself strong-minded, they said. In person she was no fairy. In manner she was not one of the graces. She was enthusiastic, quixotic, visionary, ambitious. Her masculine intellect was no judge of woman's capacities. Her robust constitution was no measure of ordinary women's health and strength and powers of endurance. It was unbecoming her sex to solicit subscriptions in person, to address public meetings, to ride all over the country with Mr. Hawks and ask for sixpenny contributions. To this "common-place ridicule" Miss Lyon simply replied: "What do I that is wrong? My heart is sick, my soul is pained with this empty gentility, this genteel nothingness. I am doing a great work. I cannot come down." It is well that she was not like ordinary women, still less like ordinary men. If she had been, she never would have founded Mt. Holyoke Seminary. If she had not been quite extraordinary both in her powers and in her virtues; if she had not been almost superhuman in her courage and strength, in her patience and perseverance, in her faith and hope, in her unselfishness and unworldliness, in her self-denial and self-sacrifice, in her consecration to the higher education of woman and to the service of the Master, in her capacity for planning and executing, for organizing and training,—she never would have accomplished the work which was given her to do. Those years in which, while associated with Miss Grant in Ipswich, she co-operated with her in assiduous but fruitless labors to endow and thus perpetuate the seminary already existing there; the years after separating from Miss Grant and leaving Ipswich, when, taking counsel with such wise counselors and such warm friends as Professor Hitchcock and Dr. Packard, she thought out, studied out, worked out and prayed out her own plan for a new seminary of which the distinguishing characteristics were to be a higher standard of education and a lower standard of expense than at any existing female seminary, and all to be controlled by the spirit of the gospel of Christ, and marked features of which were to be low salaries for the teachers, low tuition but the highest order of teaching for the pupils, and, as a means to that end, the domestic work to be performed by the members of the school,—features which called forth remonstrances even from Miss Grant and Miss Catharine Beecher, and incurred ridicule and reproach from presidents and professors, principals and teachers of fashionable schools for young ladies, doctors of divinity, professional men, and men and women of standing and influence; the years, partly of wild speculation, partly of pecuniary pressure and generally hard times for raising money (for 1837 was a year of pressure and panic in the money market), in which, with the help of Rev. Mr. Hawks and of Deacons Safford, Avery, and Porter, she raised the money for the first building (the most of it by subscriptions the largest of which was one thousand dollars and the smallest six cents, and the balance by borrowing to make up the deficiency), and then erected the northern half of the present main edifice and finished and furnished it (though it was neither finished nor furnished till after the school was opened), planning and superintending the whole and every part in person, and seeing to it that every stone and every brick was properly laid; and the year in which the seminary was opened with eighty students selected out of twice that number who applied, and sifted again and again like Gideon's army, till the cowards and laggards were all left out, and there remained only those of like spirit and purpose with herself,—such teachers as Eunice Caldwell, and such pupils as Persis Woods and Ann Webster (Mrs. Cowles, Mrs. Curtis, and Mrs Eaton), two of whom you alumnæ heard yesterday and so had an opportunity to judge for yourselves what sort of stuff primeval Holyoke was made of (Would that we also had heard! *O si nos audivissemus!*); and, we might add, the twelve years of her principalship during which she carried out her plans, expanded her ideals, impressed herself on teachers and pupils, and, though not without many trials and hardships, realized all and more than all she had ever dared to hope, in the growth and prosperity of the seminary and the manifest blessing of God upon all connected with it,—I say these years constitute the *heroic age* in the history not only of Mt. Holyoke Seminary, but of all the seminaries that have been modeled after it, and all the women's colleges that have directly or indirectly sprung from it, not only in our own country, but in each of the other three quarters of the globe.

And the wise, patient, persevering, much-wandering, much-planning, much-enduring, many-sided, all-suffering, and all-conquering Ulysses of this grand epic—our Iliad of battles and struggles and our Odyssey of conflict and victory—was Mary Lyon. Or, to use a more suitable illustration from sacred history, she was the Moses and Joshua in our history of woman's emancipation and higher education, who brought us out of the house of bondage, led us through the wilderness, and introduced us into the land of promise, the foremost among all those leaders and champions of the cause who " through faith subdued kingdoms, wrought righteousness, obtained promises, stopped the mouths of lions, out of weakness were made strong, turned to flight the armies of the aliens." And yet the crowning virtue of Miss Lyon, as of all genuine heroes, was her humility, her entire freedom from self-consciousness, and constant ascription of all she did and all she was to the providence and grace of God, which led her often and always to say with the apostle Paul, " By the grace of God I am what I am; and this grace which was bestowed upon me was not in vain; for I labored more abundantly than they all; yet not I, but the grace of God which was with me."

I have read the story over and over again at different times, and in various forms, with ever increasing interest, and never with greater wonder and delight than as it is summarily and graphically told in the semi-centennial history of our seminary, to which this anniversary has given birth. And what is even better than that, because it is imperishable and immortal, I have read her life, where she herself wrote it,— where every teacher's work should be written, where all great and good teachers always will write their greatest and best work, their life work, their autobiography,—in the hearts and lives of thousands who, directly or indirectly, have been her pupils.

I may perhaps be permitted to add that I was myself personally acquainted with Miss Lyon, and intimately associated with her, often beneath the same roof, while she was forming the plan of the seminary and raising the funds for the building, as well as during her administration of the government and instruction; and I can truly say with her last pastor, whom we are happy to see here to-day, that it was not, after all, her untiring perseverance, her executive power, or her all-embracing self-sacrificing love, though these were seldom equaled, but it was Christ formed in her and working by her that was the source of her excellence and the secret of her power; and I have never seen so perfect an instance of absolute forgetfulness of self, of entire consecration and oneness with Christ, as in the founder of this seminary.

So great was the labor of founding Mt. Holyoke Seminary and inaugurating the higher education of women : *Tantæ molis erat Romanam condere gentem!* Here was the cradle not only of Holyoke, but of all the other seminaries which graduates of Holyoke have founded, from the Nestorian and the Cherokee Seminaries to Oxford and Mills, and from Oxford and Mills to the Huguenot Seminary and her sisters, almost as numerous as the Pleiads, that cluster about her in South Africa. This is the germ of all the women's colleges from Vassar to Bryn Mawr that have sprung up in such rapid succession in the last quarter of a century : *Ubi et gentis cunabula nostræ*.

The time would fail me to speak particularly of the successors of Miss Lyon,—Miss Whitman, Miss Chapin, Miss Hopkins, Mrs. Stoddard, Miss French, Miss Ward, and Miss Blanchard, Principals; and their Associate Principals, Miss Hazen, Miss Spofford, Miss Jessup, Miss Tolman, Miss Ellis, and Miss Edwards; all taken from among the teachers of the seminary, as presidents usually should be taken from among the professors, though I always pity the professor on whom the duty is devolved; all of course in the regular line of apostolical succession from the founder, imbued with her principles, saturated with her ideas, instinct with her spirit, and intent on perfecting her work; all doing missionary work with a missionary spirit and on salaries less than those of *home* missionaries ; all more or less conservative in their ideas of government and instruction and sufficiently strenuous for a strict observance of the rules, and yet each sufficiently individual in her talents and character, independent in her methods and nobly ambitious to keep Holyoke in the front rank among the schools, and her administration foremost in the educational and the religious history of Mt. Holyoke. It is worthy of note, in answer to the alleged antagonism between the higher education of women and the institution of the family,* that out of seven principals (eight including Miss Lyon), four, after being at the head of the seminary, became heads of families, and presided over the home with no less wisdom and success than they had presided over the school. It should also be remarked as an illustration of the health and longevity of the institution, and at the same time as a cause of thanksgiving to God, that the same kind Providence which raised them up one after another to fill the office of principal, as from time to time it became vacant, has preserved the majority of them until this time and permitted so many of them to rejoice with us to-day in the ever-growing prosperity of their beloved seminary, as we greatly rejoice to welcome them here on this interesting anniversary.

We cannot so much as name the many *teachers* who have made up the faculty of instruction during these years, who have done more and better work with less pay and less grumbling, nay, with more *esprit du corps*, with more Christian gladness and singleness of heart, I verily believe, than any other corps of teachers within the range of my acquaintance; themselves promoted from the ranks of pupils, as officers

---

* On this point see also the speech of Mr. Millingen on a subsequent page and the statistics there given of the marriage of Holyoke graduates.

ANNIVERSARY EXERCISES. 117

should be and the best soldiers usually are (though this practice, like that of intermarriage among royal families, may be carried so far as to thin and chill, if not corrupt, the blood); some of whom have grown old in the office (if women and Christians ever do grow old), and yet are as enthusiastic in their work as those who have recently entered the service. In 1837 the faculty consisted of one principal, one associate principal, two teachers, and three assistant pupils, and, so far as appears from the catalogue, without any division of labor or distribution of departments. In 1887 there are over thirty teachers, each one of whom has her department of instruction and her especial work, in which she labors with the double enthusiasm inspired by the love of her particular branch of literature, science, or art, and her love for her pupils and her profession. This well illustrates not only the growth of the seminary, but the progress of science, and the advance in the higher education of women.

And now what shall I say of the two thousand graduates and four thousand non-graduates, more than six thousand in all, who have been connected with the seminary? Three-fourths of them have been teachers for a longer or a shorter time, a large proportion of them for life; we might almost say, they have all been teachers as Miss Lyon insisted that they all should be, though it were only teachers of their younger brothers and sisters. Two hundred of them have been foreign missionaries, great numbers of them wives of home missionaries; and so many of them have become wives of ministers that the seminary has sometimes been regarded as a kind of factory for the manufacture of that commodity. Not a few have been founders of Holyokes at the West and South, in Europe, in Western and Southern Asia, in South Africa, in the islands of the sea. They have been leaders in education, in religion, in temperance, in reform clubs, in societies for foreign and home missions, in public schools and Sunday-schools, in literature and science, in authorship and journalism, in church parlors and church work of every kind, in general society, and, last but not least, in intelligent and cultivated homes, where all education and all religion must begin. In short, there is a smaller percentage of drones and butterflies and aimless and therefore ignoble lives, and a larger proportion of busy bees and earnest workers, among the graduates of Mt. Holyoke Seminary than can be found in the same number of women, or men either, in any similar institution or in any other walk of life with which I am acquainted. Service is their watchword. Their motto is, *not to be ministered unto, but to minister*, and, if need be, sacrifice their lives for the good of men and the glory of God. And they are none the less attractive, personally and socially, for their solid excellences and their useful services. Indeed, it is only the most solid substances, the most compact and fine-grained materials that are capable of receiving the highest polish. There is no gem so hard as the diamond, and there is none so brilliant. Many a polished gem "of purest ray serene" shines in the humblest parsonages of our New England churches, in the homes of missionaries on the obscurest and remotest of the islands of the sea. Many a cultivated flower of rare beauty and richness adorns the abode of the home missionary on our Western prairies. There is no politeness like benevolence in little things. There is no beauty that can compare with the beauty of holiness. Many a daughter of Holyoke has carried with her into all these spheres of usefulness graces that would adorn a palace, and so has illustrated the motto of the seminary: "That our daughters may be as corner-stones polished after the similitude of a palace." And as *alma mater* welcomes so many of her daughters home at this joyful festival, and thinks of so many more who have not been able to come, methinks I hear her say: These are my jewels, these are my strength and support; these are my joy and crown of rejoicing. We believe also that as, one after another, they pass from their service to their reward, they will be among the brightest jewels in the crown of the Redeemer. And when they are all gathered in His kingdom, with them that are wise and that turn many to righteousness, they will shine as the brightness of the firmament, and as the stars forever and ever. And if *alma mater* may be indulged in any partiality for any one of her fifty classes, the older sisters will surely pardon her if she says, as the Germans say of the children in their large families: "*Das neueste das beste,*" the youngest is the best; nay, they will unanimously *approve*, and we will all with one voice join our applause, as at this semi-centennial celebration she points to the semi-centennial class with peculiar satisfaction, and puts especial honor on the class that graduates to-day.

You will perhaps expect me to say something of the trustees on this occasion. But the fact is, there is not much to *be* said. Our duties are not arduous; our responsibilities are not weighty. Like the poor Indian preacher who, when told that his compensation was poor pay, replied that his preaching was poor preaching, our service is almost as small as our salaries. We come together once a year to see the train moving smoothly and safely on the track and bearing us along with it with scarcely a touch from our hands. For, like the trustees of our literary institutions generally, we are most of us passengers and figure-heads, not the engine or the engineers, not the workmen or the moving power. But we always feel that it is good for us to be here, for here we stand on holy ground, the air we breathe is holy, and we go away better than we came.

But there have always been some of our number who are anything but figure-heads or mere passengers. There were those good ministers, Mr. Hawks, President Hitchcock, and Dr. Kirk, who bore the heat and burden of the day and labored in season and out of season in the founding of the seminary, for the shaping of its course, or for the spiritual welfare of its pupils; and those I had almost said better deacons, Safford, Porter, Avery, Kingman, Williston, Sawyer, Hitchcock and others, who have put their shoulders to the wheel and been both working and moving powers, who, as Lord Bacon says of himself, have been willing to be "operatives, carriers of wood, and drawers of water," provided only they could subserve the interests of the seminary and the good of mankind; and, best of all, the better halves of these good deacons, deaconesses in a double sense, two of whom I cannot but name, Mrs. Safford and Mrs. Porter, who, in addition to personal services and pecuniary contributions, had two homes, their own homestead and the seminary, in both of which they watched over and cared for Holyoke teachers and pupils as if they had been their own daughters.

Nor can I fail, as the representative of the seminary on this occasion, to allude to the pecuniary benefactors of the institution—the contributors for the erection of the main building, from the first subscribers of a thousand dollars each, Daniel Safford and Samuel Williston, to the poor widows whose two mites outweighed all the rest in the balances of the sanctuary; the war governor who started, and the others who completed, the donation for the gymnasium, and the young lady, then a member of the senior class, afterwards a teacher in the seminary, whose composition gave the first impulse to the contribution; the founder of the Tolman fund, our Horsford fund in embryo and on a small scale; the contributors to the Education Fund, chiefly Phebe Hazeltine, Homer Merriam, Edward Smith, and E. A. Goodnow; the founders and donors of our General Fund, especially John B. Eldredge and Eber Gridley; the giver of the Durant Library, who cannot but greatly rejoice to-day to see what her munificent donation of books has grown to; the donor and builder of Williston Hall and the Memorial Observatory (thank God for his recovery, and his presence with us to-day); and the giver of Goodnow Park, who, by his recent gift of Goodnow Hall to the Huguenot Seminary in South Africa, one of the fairest of Holyoke's daughters, has pleased and honored the mother scarcely less than the daughter. Nor can I forget the missionary graduates who have contributed so largely to the scientific collections; the ladies and gentlemen, and classes of alumnæ whose gifts have enriched the Art Gallery; least of all can I forget those unfailing and inexhaustible benefactors of the seminary in every period of its history, the undergraduates and their teachers, whose contributions and solicitations have supplied the steam-heating apparatus, built the water tower, put in the elevator and provided means for I know not how many improvements, repairs, and additions to the facilities of education. After all, we are obliged to say that the largest benefactor of the seminary is that dear and good old lady, the Commonwealth of Massachusetts, who came to its relief in an emergency with a gift of $40,000, which was used, first for the payment of a debt, and then for enlargement of our educational means and resources; and I am proud and happy to say that since that time the institution has never owed any man anything, except the debt of gratitude and love, which of course never *can* be fully paid. Alas that we cannot add to this list of benefactions and benefactors a jubilee foundation as ample as the Horsford, which would give all our hard-worked and poorly paid teachers once in seven years a year's absence for recreation and improvement, and several endowments of professorships (we have not so much as one) for our teachers who have so well earned the title of professors. I do not know of any institution where a moderate endowment of professorships is so well deserved or would do so much good. We are profoundly grateful that our former principal, with the co-operation of our Alumnæ Associations, has at length succeeded in completing the Mary Lyon Fund for the endowment of the principalship, though she had to raise it in the old way, with much solicitation, and for the most part in comparatively small sums. We only wonder that some wealthy and benevolent man or woman did not come forward and claim the privilege of giving it all in a lump. But perhaps this is the more appropriate way. Certainly it repeats more nearly the experience of Mary Lyon herself. No doubt He who sat over against the treasury in Jerusalem applauded these smaller gifts as He did those in the days of his incarnation, and He who fed the multitudes with a few loaves and fishes will, in his own wonder-working way, bless these gifts and increase their value a hundred and a thousand fold.

Now I have no time left to speak of a subject which I at one time thought of making the theme of my whole discourse, viz.: the ideas and principles which our seminary represents and embodies. For it is ideas that mark and make epochs. It is principles that create institutions, and institutions in their turn perpetuate principles. Ideas and principles give *life* to institutions that will not die; and institutions that deserve to live and will live are the embodiment of principles and ideas. Men die, but institutions live. This is the fundamental reason, the *raison d'être*, the reason for the existence of Mt. Holyoke Seminary. The founder of our seminary was, beyond any other woman that I ever knew, a woman of ideas and principles, and she became the founder of this institution simply as a means of incorporating and perpetuating those principles and ideas. May I simply enunciate in the briefest possible form a few of the ideas that seem to me to be especially incorporated in this seminary.

1. That of an *institution* with a board of trustees, a permanent faculty of instruction, and a fixed course of studies; with suitable buildings and grounds, with proper endowments and permanent funds, with library and laboratories and apparatus and collections, with all the facilities and means of education, not just the same, but just as ample and suitable for educating young women, as are furnished for educating young men,—for giving young women not just the same education, but just as good an education as young men can get in our best colleges and universities. This whole idea, and every particular that I have enumerated was disputed, repudiated, ridiculed, before this seminary was founded. But now the idea and all the particulars are settled principles and established facts; and the credit of settling them belongs to Mt. Holyoke Seminary.

2. The idea of a family organization to which all the teachers and all the pupils belong, of which the principal is the head and the teachers are older and the pupils younger sisters, in which the interest of one is the interest of all, and the well-being and well-doing of all is the concern of every one; in which, as in the Greek and Roman state, the unit is not the individual or the class, but the family, not a part but a whole, in which every individual must labor and suffer and sacrifice more or less for the general good; in which, as in other families, for the health, wealth, comfort, and convenience of the family as well as for

the benefit of each individual, the domestic work is performed more or less by every member; whereby, in short, the dignity of labor, the happiness of service, the blessedness of self-denial and sacrifice, the old-fashioned virtues of industry, economy, and system, and the law of mutual and equal love are taught by precept and example, until they are incorporated in the whole spirit and soul and body of the individual, even as they are embodied in the institution itself. In the letters of alumnæ, which constitute not the least valuable and not the least interesting part of our semi-centennial history, next to the educational advantages and the Christian character and influence of the seminary, the writers insist most earnestly on the value of the family organization and the domestic work, as furnishing a daily object-lesson in system, order, industry, and economy. They speak of it as exhibiting a beautiful and successful example of co-operative housekeeping; they emphasize it as teaching the dignity of labor and exemplifying both the prose and the poetry of housekeeping in the family; they glorify it as illustrating and enforcing the duty and the privilege of sacrifice and service one to another and each to all in the common relations of every-day life. More than one of the writers declare it to be the chief glory of Mt. Holyoke that she has taught this so-much-needed lesson. And Dr. Kirk expressed the same opinion to me as we sat under the trees near Miss Lyon's grave one day and discussed the question, What were the most characteristic features of Mt. Holyoke Seminary.

3. The idea of a Christian institution in which the Bible is a prominent text-book, the rule of truth and duty, the touch-stone of character and life; while every teacher is a living epistle of Christ and every pupil a sacred trust to be educated for the Master ; the buildings, the grounds, the lecture rooms, the apparatus, the collections, the funds, all given by Christian men and women and sacred to Christ and the Church ; and the teachers and pupils all taught to feel that to be benevolent, to be Christ-like, to be Christian at all times and in all the relations of life, is the highest style of man. Or, as Miss Lyon used to express the idea, making use of her favorite text in Ezekiel and her favorite illustration (Ezek. 43 : 12): "This is the law of the house; upon the top of the mountain the whole limit thereof round about shall be most holy ; behold this is the law of the house."

4. A high standard of scholarship and large advantages for education combined with low salaries and small expenses, board and tuition being furnished at cost, only $60 a year at the beginning, only $110 on an average ; and when, in order to meet increasing expenses and raise the standard of education, it became necessary to increase salaries and tuition, not the trustees or the students, but the teachers were the party to object. Here again the principles of industry and economy, of sacrifice and service, come in, and they prove to be an inexhaustible mine of financial, as well as moral and religious, resources. To love our neighbor as ourselves has been shown to be a *golden* rule in the worldly as well as the religious sense. Godliness has been proved to be profitable for all things, having the promise of the life that now is as well as of that which is to come. Other schools, more richly en-

dowed, have had their ups and downs, have suffered for want of students and want of means, but Mt. Holyoke has had an unfailing resource in itself, in the unselfishness of its faculty and students. If we had had more ample endowments, we could have done more and better work, but we never have a deficit, we almost always have a small surplus sufficient to meet an exigency, to supply a felt want, to provide a needed improvement. Pressure, panic, debt, embarrassment, are words not to be found in our dictionary; and we recommend the system—the idea at least and the principle—to employers and employed in these days of strikes, pools, and Knights of Labor.

5. As to the grade and growth of the institution, the school at Ipswich was at first announced as the model and standard, but the seminary soon outgrew the model in its requirements for admission, in the strictness of the entrance examinations, in the extent and fixedness of the curriculum, in the number, character, and attainments of its faculty and students, almost as much as it exceeded it in buildings, funds, and facilities of education. Progress, not less than holiness to the Lord, was the law of the house; both, as our semi-centennial history says, were inscribed on every brick by the hand of the founder, as Nebuchadnezzar stamped his name on every brick of great Babylon which he builded. Steady growth and strict economy were wrought together in its foundations, and incorporated in the whole structure. Miss Lyon's idea, as she expressed it, was to found a seminary which was to furnish an education so good that the daughters of the wealthy could obtain nothing better, while the daughters of the middle classes would be able to meet all its expenses and enjoy all its advantages. "My thoughts have turned," she writes, "not to the higher, not to the poorer, but to the middle classes; these contain the main-springs and wheels that move the world." These words of the founder define the sphere of the seminary; these prescribe its work; do not these also fix its grade and determine its name? This is not the place to discuss the question of a change of name. Far be it from me to dictate, or to anticipate, the action of alumnæ or trustees, on a subject about which the friends of the seminary differ. But there are some points in regard to which it seems to me we must all be agreed. None of us wish the seminary to be called what it is not. Better, *far* better *to be* a college without being called so, than to be called a college without fully deserving the name. If we call it a college, we must make it so, we must be prepared to furnish all which the name demands—more work, more teachers, more money, more buildings; we must be able to meet all which it implies. None of us, I presume, wish to *part* with the name which was given it by its founder, which the alumnæ bear on their diplomas, under which it has won its victories and accomplished its work. "*In hoc signo vincemus.*" Under this standard we have triumphed, by this sign we shall conquer. None of us wish to abandon our work, to relinquish our sphere, to forsake our constituency, to lose our old name. It is not uprooting and transplanting that we want, but growth. May not our post-graduate or extended and extra under-graduate course, which we owe to the wisdom of Miss Ward and the culture of Miss Blanchard and Miss Edwards,

furnish the solution? Let that course have its natural and normal growth, and when we have students who have completed a college curriculum, and are entitled to a college diploma (as I am inclined to think we may have very soon, sooner than the public or the friends of the seminary are aware), the legislature will not withhold from us the right to confer the degree, and the trustees will not be slow to confer it. In other words, let us superadd a collegiate department, let us give it hearty encouragement and support, so that all who are anxious for a college diploma, and are willing to earn it, may have the opportunity; and then—although in my own view the name is of comparatively little consequence, still, if it be the wish of the faculty and the alumnæ, especially if any one will give us a hundred thousand or half a million dollars—we will add to our existing name college and whatever else may best express the then existing facts in the case. But let us hold on to our seminary, with its natural growth, of course, and such changes as the times may demand, but with substantially the present curriculum. Let the institution continue to be and be called Mt. Holyoke Seminary; let it grow by striking its roots deeper and spreading its branches wider, and thus lifting itself higher rather than try to raise it mechanically into another sphere called by another name; just as the grand and graceful old elms of our Connecticut valley not only grow, but in growing gradually lift themselves bodily, trunk and roots, as well as branches, not out of the ground but above it, still rooted in the soil in which they were planted and from which they draw their nourishment.

A college education, for young women as for young men, is for the few; Mt. Holyoke Seminary is for the many. Its sphere is the middle classes, its work is to leaven the masses with intelligence, virtue, and piety, until the whole is leavened. Let it aspire not to do everything, but whatever it undertakes to do, do it well; not to be a university and teach everything, but to be, in a broad sense, in the highest and best sense, a normal school, and train teachers who shall teach everybody; teachers for the middle and the laboring classes; teachers not only for Smith and Wellesley, but especially for Northfield (we want more schools like Northfield and Mt. Hermon, and we shall have them too); teachers for the high schools and the public schools generally (the public schools are now chiefly in the hands of women, and if these schools are ever to be elevated and made Christian, it must be under the influence of such seminaries as Mt. Holyoke); teachers for Sunday-schools and Bible classes (Miss Lyon urged the addition of a fourth year to the course that there might be time and room for more Latin and Greek and Hebrew, and she often said that the time would come when Bible class teachers would feel that they must study the Scriptures in the original languages); teachers for industrial schools (industrial schools are the great desideratum and the increasingly felt want of our age and country, and Mt. Holyoke is not only a normal school to furnish just the teachers for such schools, but it is itself a model and ideal industrial school, illustrating the ideas, the principles, and the spirit, largely the methods also in which they should be conducted); Christian teachers and Christian workers for the toiling and surging, the voting and ruling multitudes of our great and growing republic; Christian teachers and Christian workers for the suffering and perishing millions of the nominally Christian, Mohammedan and Pagan world. This is the great want, not only of our age and country but of our world; and Mt. Holyoke and her numerous offshoots and other seminaries like them are just the institutions to supply the want. It is not the province even of the university, as that profound thinker, Dr. Mulford, well remarks, to make discoveries in art, science, and philosophy, so much as to teach and train those who shall make such discoveries. Such I take to be the province of our seminary, to teach the teachers, to train the trainers, to educate the educators, the discoverers, the leaders, whose discoveries, labors, and influence will shape the masses in the generations that are to come. Let us magnify this office. At the same time let us not be caught by the captivating bait of a merely practical education. Let us hold on to the old, long-tried disciplinary studies. Mathematics are the archetype of nature and the framework of the universe. The Creator himself geometrizes, as Plato says. And Pythagoras still earlier taught that number is the first principle of all things on earth and in the starry heavens. Language and literature are the humanities; they broaden the views, enlarge the sympathies, and enrich the mind with a knowledge of human nature, with the wisdom of the ages. With all her new departures, when Harvard wanted an orator for her quarter-millennial celebration, she had to take Mr. Lowell; and when the orator pleaded for the old learning, the humanities, the classics, the Greek, he was himself the living demonstration of his doctrine. The orator at the semi-centennial celebration of Columbia College was equally earnest and eloquent in his advocacy of classical studies.

Literature, science, and art offer to our graduates wide and inviting fields; the professions also are no longer closed against them; the medical profession especially opens to them a sphere of almost unlimited extent which greatly needs the service of educated women, and to which they are peculiarly adapted. In or out of the pulpit, also, there is ample room and a loud call for more lay preaching and women's teaching. The morals, the manners, and the arguments of the bar would be greatly improved by a slight infusion of feminine moral suasion and Holyoke Christian spirit; and, for that matter, clerical manners and pulpit eloquence would not be injured by a suffusion of the same spirit. Even in politics, a little *more* "intimidation" from the gentler sex would do no harm. Journalism and the press generally will be refined, and popular education will be exalted as educated women are beginning to find a place on school boards and school committees, and to control these fountains of influence. The presence of cultivated Christian women in offices, shops, and stores is destined to elevate and purify all kinds of business in the times to come. It is preeminently the prerogative of such women to guide and form public sentiment in all matters of purity and propriety, manners and morals, temperance, and religion. Above all, the influence of cultivated Christian women is needed to beautify and sanctify the home, to penetrate and pervade all the walks of private and social, and thus, indirectly, of public life. Thus for women as well as men now the field is the world; it is all now wide open even to the deep recesses of the Dark Continent.

The difficulty now lies not in the finding of an open field, but in the selection. No word of Horace Greeley has been more frequently quoted, or more potent in its influence, than that short and pithy saying, "Young man, go West." The same advice may well be given to young women, who wish to know how and where they can make the most of themselves, and best serve the Master, the Church, their country, and mankind. Mrs. Banister gave her last years, and some of the best work of her life, to an organized effort for sending female teachers to the West. What graduate of Mt. Holyoke will take up her mantle, and carry on the work upon a larger scale, and under the pressure of a new and more urgent necessity? Who will plant a Holyoke Seminary in every State west of the Mississippi, and organize a Holyoke Alumnæ Association on the Pacific Coast? Who will sow Christian schools of every kind broadcast over the whole wide field of Mormondom, and thus achieve a conquest which baffles the wisdom and power of the national government? What educated Christian woman would not do all she can to right the wrongs of her sex in Utah, and emancipate her sisters from a bondage worse than African slavery? What daughter of Mary Lyon will not do her best for Home Missions, and the New West Commission? Young woman, go West.

If any field can compete with the West in its claims just at this time, it is the South. Much is said nowadays, and justly said, of "the New West." The New South is a word of equal significance, of no less right and power to command a willing and devoted service. The South has at length awaked from her long sleep, cast off her pride and pleasure and scorn of labor, and gone to work. The New South is advancing in agriculture, in manufactures, in education, in industrial schools for both colors and both sexes, with such gigantic strides that Northern capital and enterprise begin to fear the competition; and New England piety and philanthropy may well look to her honors, and see that no one take her crown. The South has created a new literature since the war. Society and politics will be the last to feel the renovating influence. But that change will surely come, is already coming. I cannot say that the South no longer looks with suspicion upon teachers, preachers, and Christian helpers from the North. But there is a broad and promising field there which is wide open now, and opening wider every day, for wise co-operation with the New South in their rapidly advancing educational and Christian work. And I would like to be remembered as saying to graduates and undergraduates of Holyoke at this semi-centennial celebration, Young woman, go South. The field is large and white for the harvest. Who will reap it? Who will plant schools and seminaries like Holyoke all over the South? And then at our next semi-centennial, when delegates come from the East and the West and the North and the South, we will welcome especially the representatives of the Alumnæ Association of the South, and say to them: "Many daughters have done virtuously, but thou excellest them all."

But why make comparisons? Why prescribe limits? Go into all the world and preach the gospel to every creature. Go to the New Japan. Go to old China, and make it new. Go everywhere, and make all things new. It is the work which God is doing fast every day, and in which he calls you to his help. Go where the field is the widest, and the harvest the whitest. Go where you are most needed, and where others are most unwilling to go. That is the command of the Master. That is the call of the gospel. That is the way of Mt. Holyoke Seminary. That is the spirit in which the Principal of the Huguenot Seminary, thus early in its history, is rallying all the South-African schools to the invasion and conquest of the Dark Continent. And who shall hinder "the sweet influence of the Pleiades"! No, let there be no limitation. For women as well as men, I repeat it, the world is now open in all its parts and in every department, and with what wonder and delight must the founder of this seminary, amidst a cloud of witnesses, look down upon her "dear daughters," and see them entering in and taking possession of every part of it, in the secular as well as the sacred sphere, in the spirit of missionaries, under the influence of benevolent motives, for the sake of doing good. Can there be a better work, a higher sphere, a loftier ambition than this?

Americans have a passion for high-sounding titles. The primary school wants to be a high school, the high school aspires to be an academy, the academy claims to be a college, and the college calls itself a university. Nay, the preparatory school, particularly the private school, dubs itself a university. Of 1,588 "institutions for *secondary* instruction," reported by the Commissioner of Education for 1883–84, there are seven with the pretentious title of "university," and 127 with the ambitious name of "college"; and of 370 institutions reported as colleges and universities, 123 style themselves "universities." Six of our states have 49 "universities"—more than double the number in the whole German empire! In view of such facts may I not repeat and emphasize what I have already said: Better, far better to be a college without being called so, than to be called a college without deserving the name. Meanwhile the bottom is in danger of dropping out of our whole system of education. Daniel Webster is credited with saying, that there is always room enough in the upper stories. There certainly is, or is likely to be, room enough in the lower stories of our educational system. There is room, and there is a future for those institutions which are modest enough to call themselves what they are, and wise enough to choose the middle and lower stories. There is any number of so-called colleges of all sorts and sizes scattered all over the country, but there is, there can be, only one Mt. Holyoke, as there can be only one Washington. Surely no other name can be more exalted, none so sacred as this. Can any of us doubt that at the end of the next half century, as now at the end of this, and more and more as the centuries roll away and the millennium draws near, those who are educated on this consecrated eminence will count it their highest honor to be known as the graduates of Mt. Holyoke Seminary?

Standing on this high post of observation between the centuries, from which, like the heroes and prophets of Homer's verse, we can see both "backward and forward" and infer the future with more or less confidence from the past; while we look back upon the past with wonder and gratitude, we cannot but look forward to the future with courage and hope. There are indeed portentous signs, great agitations and commotions, distress of nations, conflict of classes, upheavals of society and government, nation threatening war against nation, and sometimes it seems as if one half of Europe was preparing to precipitate itself upon the other half, and as if all the energies and resources of the civilized world were enlisted in contriving engines and forces for mutual destruction. But God reigns. Christ is at the helm. The head of the church is head over all things for the church, and all power on earth and in heaven is in his hands. I repeat every day of my life the words of that familiar hymn, and often I sing them to my own heart in the darkness of the night:—

> "This God is the God we adore,
> Our faithful, unchangeable friend,
> Whose love is as large as his power,
> And neither knows measure nor end.
>
> "'Tis Jesus, the first and the last,
> Whose spirit shall guide us safe home;
> We'll praise him for all that is past,
> And trust him for all that's to come."

We are astonished, almost dazed, as we review the changes of the last half century. But they have been changes for the better. And the changes of the next half century will doubtless be greater and better still. These changes and commotions are the very footsteps of his coming, who has said in his word and is now saying, to us in his providence: "Behold I make all things new." For education and religion, for the church and the world, "Our trust is in God"—God in Christ reconciling the world unto himself; even as in the darkest hour of our dreadful civil war we proclaimed our trust in Him and stamped it indelibly on our coins, and did not trust in vain. And under God my hope is largely in the higher education, further development and wider influence of woman, which is so marked a characteristic of the age. Civilization has always advanced in the world just in proportion to the ascendency of woman among the nations and the ages. And in no age and no nation has that ascendency been so marked as in our own. Buckle, the historian of civilization, with all his one-sided exaltation of physical science and material forces, sees in the higher education and growing influence of woman the promise of a great advancement in science;* not because women have been them-

---
* See his Address before "The Royal Institution," Miscellaneous Works, Vol. 1. p. 1.

selves the greatest discoverers, scientists, and artists of this or any age, but they have been the mothers and the educators of great discoverers. Great men have usually had great and good mothers and have derived from them, as mothers and early educators, the intuitive ideas, the imaginative faculties, the emotional natures, the moral and religious feelings and impulses which distinguish the sex, which usually distinguish great men and make them great. The genius and eloquence, the faith and love and power of Chrysostom and Augustine existed first in their mothers, Nonna and Monica. So the Apostle Paul, when he called to remembrance the unfeigned faith of Timothy, could not forget that it dwelt first in his grandmother Lois and his mother Eunice. Washington was largely indebted to Mary and Martha Washington for what he was and what he achieved. The social, in other words the feminine, side has generally been largely developed in authors, orators, and statesmen who have done the most to shape society and government. Feminine features are conspicuous in the very faces of such poets and men of genius as Shakespeare and Milton, even as feminine elements blend harmoniously with masculine in their characters and lives.

A recent German author has advanced the theory that the Semitic race, which, beyond either the Greek, the Roman, or the Teutonic, has been the world's educator, is the ever-feminine (ewigweibliche) factor, in other words the receptive, spiritual, monotheistic, religious, believing element among the nations. A marvelous union of womanly tenderness with manly courage and strength is characteristic of the traditional portraits of Him who was the Son of Man and at the same time the Son of God, as also of the most admired conceptions and representations of Him by the great masters of modern painting and sculpture. And—with reverence be it said—we reach the highest and most just conception of our Heavenly Father only when we conceive of him as uniting the fullness of a father's with the tenderness of a mother's love for his erring and imperfect children. The equal and harmonious blending of woman's influence with that of man—so unlike the seclusion of the sex in the Orient and in ancient history—is the aim and effort, nay, it is already the characteristic feature of the age, and it is the most hopeful sign of our times. The brightest and best reigns in English history, aye, and in the history of the world from Semiramis to our own day, have been the reigns of female sovereigns. Queen Elizabeth, Queen Anne, Queen Victoria—these are the names which represent the most brilliant epochs in the literature, the society, the government of our Mother Country, and the happiest periods in the lives of the English people. Only compare the reign of Victoria with the reign of the Four Georges and William the Fourth; God bless her! she was the friend of our country in the hour of our supreme necessity; and her whole vast empire, on which the sun never sets, which belts the globe and contains one-fourth of its entire population, is the empire of liberty and law, of justice and philanthropy. Her reign runs parallel with the history of Mt. Holyoke Seminary; this very week her people celebrate the fiftieth anniversary of her reign, as we celebrate the semi-centennial of our Queen. Both celebrations represent the coronation, the reign, the sovereignty of woman; and the sovereignty of woman is the sovereignty of the people with their better half in the ascendency. Normally, and as a general fact actually, the reign of woman is the reign of gentleness, of goodness, of purity, of piety, of temperance, of peace, of charity, of philanthropy, of love, of all the graces and virtues. The sway of woman is generally by tact, that is by *delicate touch*, by good taste and good sense, by personal and social attraction, by moral and religious persuasion, by intuitive wisdom, by subtle and refined and therefore irresistible influence. Of course there are exceptions, but they are so manifestly abnormal that they prove the rule. The best things always become the worst, when they are perverted. Aristotle says, man properly educated and trained is the best of animals, but if uneducated, he becomes the worst of them all. This is doubly, trebly true of woman. She must be properly educated and normally developed. She must know herself, she must understand her sphere, she must feel her responsibilities, she must make the most of the best there is in her.

Victor Hugo says, "The nineteenth century is woman's century." The twentieth century will be more so. I would like to live in it and through it. I expect to see it, to look down upon it from a higher sphere. The Apostle John saw it, or a bright and beautiful image of it, in prophetic vision. He says, "I saw an angel standing in the sun." I do not know what the commentators make of that. But I know what it signifies to me. It signifies the educated, sanctified, Christian womanhood of this and the coming age. It aptly symbolizes woman when she has added to her faith virtue, and to her virtue knowledge. It fitly represents woman, enlightened, sanctified, and exalted to her proper sphere. And the next vision in the Apocalypse is the millennium, Satan bound a thousand years, and the New Jerusalem coming down from God out of heaven prepared as a bride adorned for her husband. And then, behold, the tabernacle of God is with men, and he will be their God, and they shall be his people, and God himself shall be with them, and be their God; and he will wipe away all tears from their eyes; for the former things are passed away.

Such is the paradise lost in Eden, regained on Calvary, begun on earth and consummated in heaven, which the promises and the providence of God authorize us to expect, and whose coming, in the light of such a semi-centennial as this, we are encouraged to hope, will not be long delayed.

The following hymn written for the occasion was sung by the seminary choir:

JUBILEE HYMN.

By REV. SAMUEL F. SMITH, D.D.

Author of " My country, 'tis of thee."

FAIR seat of learning ! who shall tell
  The joy we feel in greeting thee
On this glad day, thy festal day,
  Thy blessed day of jubilee?

O born of faith ! O nursed in prayer !
  What grateful throngs repeat thy name ;
What memories lingering round the globe,
  What fervent blessings crown thy fame ;

O loyal hearts, bring hymns of praise
  To him to whom all praise is due ;
With loyal homage pay your vows,
  In loyal faith your vows renew.

Glory to him who planned, who guides,
  The years elapsed, the years to be ;
For his dear sake, in his dear name,
  We keep our hallowed jubilee.

Diplomas were distributed by Dr. Seelye with the following words:—

Young Ladies of the Senior Class: Could there be anything better than this rain ? Could there be anything more beautifully typical of Mt. Holyoke Seminary, or more fit for this anniversary, than these blessed showers, in their fruitfulness for the needy earth,—a symbol of God's infinite mercy who makes the wilderness and the solitary place to rejoice and the desert to blossom as the rose? Blessed be he for the rain, a type of what this seminary has been in the past, and a herald of the blessings which are still to come from the over-arching heavens and the over-burdened clouds upon this Christian institution ! We hold the rain as the harbinger of hope.

It is my privilege and high pleasure, young ladies, to present to you these testimonials of your having completed your course in this institution. The testimonials themselves are of very little worth. The letters in which they are written may at any time and will at some time be obliterated. Certainly the parchment upon which they are inscribed will be destroyed. But that for which the testimonials bear witness, written upon your heart, engraven as with a pen of iron and the point of a diamond, is not to fade ; shall grow brighter as you go forward toward the fulfillment of that which has been done for you and by you and with you through these four years.

I congratulate you that you have spent your years of seminary life in Mt. Holyoke, where things are taught that are real, where education is based upon realities of character and life. Mt. Holyoke Seminary, the queen of all our institutions for the higher education of women, at first received the crown and still retains the glory of seeking first the kingdom of God and his righteousness, with the confident expectation that if this be gained all other things shall be added thereto.

I have only to exhort you, in these closing hours, to keep fast hold of that which you have here received. "Hold fast that thou hast that no man take thy crown." Do not be ashamed of the faith with which you have been inspired. Do not fail to hold it as more priceless than all the knowledge you have received or shall attain. Let it be the crown of your life and the glory of your blessed experience in this earthly state as it is the fulfillment of our hopes for you in the heavenly kingdom. It is my pleasure to present to you with these diplomas also my heartiest congratulations.

The diplomas having been presented, the following hymn, written by Harriet L. Bruce of the graduating class, was sung by the seminary choir:—

> O, HOLY King, if aught there be
> Of beauty in the passing days,
> We yield it lovingly to Thee,—
> A humble tribute to Thy praise.
>
> The passing days, the fleeting years,
> Have proved Thy wondrous power to bless,
> And evermore Thy help appears,
> To shield from harm our helplessness.
>
> O thou whose blessing is so free,
> Accept the loyal praise we sing,
> For every heart would worship Thee,
> And glory in the Lord our King.

Rev. Dr. Judson Smith offered the closing prayer:—

Almighty God, our Heavenly Father, unto Thee we lift our hearts in gratitude and praise, and seek from Thee at this hour Thy blessing, that the scene, the hour, the thoughts that have been awakened, may be sanctified unto us and may redound to Thy glory. We bless Thee for Thy providence and Thy guiding hand which have been so signally displayed in the planting and the growth of this seminary of learning. We praise Thee for that course of events toward which our thoughts have been directed this morning, by which out of weakness and in the face of great opposition and ignorance this has been developed, and which shows Thy hand in it all; that grace was bountifully given unto her with whom the thought and the beginning of this work were placed; that Thy benediction has fallen upon all who from the beginning have been associated in the work of instruction or in the direction of affairs here. We praise Thee also that the great multitude who have gathered here as students have received here those impressions which have led them to devote themselves to scenes of manifold labor by which they have been able to bear precious blessings and to glorify God in all parts of the earth. We praise Thee that facilities have been added so that as the years have passed growth has come in every desirable respect; that opportunities are multiplying and opportunities for usefulness are increasing from year to year, so that on this fiftieth anniversary the thoughts of those who preside over its affairs, its instructors, its trustees, its alumnæ, look out to a future even greater, more abundant in the things that glorify God and bless mankind. Thy blessing, Lord, has been the strength and the glory of this institution thus far. Abide with it continually in the days to come. Guide in all its plans, attend all its labors, being present ever with the teachers and pupils here and with those who go from these halls, that everywhere the training, the culture, and the character developed here may be devoted to the highest uses, to the things that multiply blessings in the earth, that diffuse sweetness and light, that overcome the powers of darkness and evil, and that give promise of the happy day to which we all look forward when the kingdoms of the earth and the learning of the earth and all its forces shall be devoted unto the kingdom of the Most High.

Let a blessing rest on these Thy young servants who have received these testimonials of completed studies here and go with them in their several ways and grant to them each a life so consecrated to Thee and to worthy living that whether it be longer or shorter it may be worthy, and may witness, wherever they may be, for righteousness and truth among men.

And be Thou, Lord, we pray Thee, with all similar schools of learning, and grant in this wondrous age when the privileges of the higher education are so wonderfully increasing and the young women of the land in so great numbers are entering into these higher privileges and advantages, grant that they may be ready for the fields of service that wait the laborer and that we may all feel that it is for such a time that these institutions and their pupils have come into the Kingdom. And widely, Lord, by the labors and the lives of these young women and of the educated youth of our land may Thy Gospel be proclaimed, the realm of darkness narrowed, the realm of light increased until Thy Kingdom shall come and Thy will be done in earth as it is in heaven. And unto the Father, the Son, and the Holy Ghost shall be praise forevermore. Amen.

The anthem "Jubilate Deo" was sung by the choir, and the benediction was pronounced by Rev. Thomas Snell Smith of Ceylon.

THURSDAY AFTERNOON.

THE exercises began at 2 o'clock, Henry D. Hyde, Esq., of the Board of Trustees, presiding.

OPENING ADDRESS OF MR. HYDE.

Miss Blanchard and Alumnæ, Young Ladies of the Graduating Class, and Gentlemen :—

IT is a pleasure afforded us all to be permitted to meet here to-day. And although the heavens seem in a measure to be unpropitious, yet as has well been said from the heavens come our numerous blessings. The anniversary we celebrate to-day is one of no ordinary importance. In fact, the grouping in this week of jubilees is unknown in the previous history of the world. Fifty years ago two young women set out in life, entered upon a career, the history and the knowledge of which have gone out through all the world. And while we speak with reverence of Victoria we speak with love and affection of Mary Lyon. And if it be a great thing that through the kind Providence that is over us all, the Queen of England has seen her possessions grow in all this half century, and has been permitted this week to have greetings come to her from subjects throughout the world, it is of no less moment that we meet here to celebrate the work that has been done in this seminary and to speak in reverence and affection of Mary Lyon, its founder. The Queen was born a queen; she but inherited by the laws of entail. Mary Lyon was no less born a queen, in the hill town in the county above here, and her life was consecrated to a new and great work. She had more faith than opportunity, as it seemed, but she made faith control the opportunity, till at last this seminary was reared, till at last a new impulse was sent throughout the civilized world, till at last the education of women was brought to the front, commanding the attention and respect, not merely of her own sex, but of men and of the church over the world. To-day we meet to celebrate the result of that little beginning and to tell of those things that have taken place within those fifty years; to recall the events of those years; to comprehend something of the progress that has been made.. When Mary Lyon began her work here the telegraph, as we now have it, was unknown, the telephone had not been dreamed of, and a thousand things have been brought in that had no existence then. Think of all that has taken place! And yet we may say with confidence that the greatest progress that has been made, take it all in all, has been the progress that was started on this hill and that has given to almost every state in the Union a daughter of Mt. Holyoke, and brought you here to testify what that progress is, and what it means in the present time, and what it is to mean in the future before us. It does not seem possible, sometimes, that the next fifty years will show the progress that the last fifty have. It seems impossible that we should expect as much of these five times ten years as we have seen in the past, and yet, when we look about us, when we consider how many lights have been kindled from this one torch, we can but believe that whoever shall gather here fifty years hence, although there may not be a single eye that ever rested on the form of Mary Lyon, or an ear that listened to her voice, yet some of you will be here who are here to-day, and you will come back to testify to the glory of this institution and what it has wrought in the fifty years which are now to come and which will be years of reminiscence as the past fifty are to-day. It is something more than ordinary that' brings us here to-day. To how many of you are there clustering recollections and associations. To the class that graduates it is a looking forward; to the most of you it is a recalling of the past, a day of recollection. Many of you can recall something of her who consecrated her life to the idea that is embodied here. Many of you cannot recall her form, yet you can recall those who succeeded her so worthily and who have borne her standard of education from the time of its foundation until the present. You come back rejoicing in the acquaintances you made here, filled with thankfulness for the instruction you received, and we welcome you back thankful for what you have done since you left this institution and that the world rises up to call you and your efforts blessed. It is said that the Queen's domain is so vast that with the rising sun the drum beats to greet her all round the world. If that be true, as it may be, it is also true that the songs of the church, the hymns of the church, the hymns of salvation go round the world not only where the English language is spoken, but in every spoken language, by the assistance of the graduates of this institution. By their aid the cross of Christ has been planted in every land, and it is something to rejoice over that in front of the drum-beat of England goes the song of Christian praise, and that it has been possible for England's power to have been extended as it has because before the army, before the Englishman, there has been the missionary of the cross to tell the story, not merely of this institution, but that great uplifting story that belongs to all our lives, if we will accept it as it comes to us.

I have said that this is a day of reminiscence to you. There are some of us also to whom it is a day of reminiscence. Some of us were educated in a sister institution across the mountains, and again and again in the days gone by we used to come here to visit, and as I crossed the mountains with His Excellency the Governor to-day, I was able to point out to him the milestones by which we measured our distance from Amherst to South Hadley. I could tell him the hour when we ought to be at the top of the mountain, and then when my eye fell on such a point I knew that in one hour I should be due at the gate! And yet with all this vividness of recollection, after a quarter of a century I could not recall a single instant of the time it took to return! Professor Tyler said that when this institution was founded there were many men who doubted its wisdom because it would surely bring many changes if it succeeded. Many of us are here to witness that those changes have come. We are not here contending against them but to show that, as those good men prophesied, so it has been fulfilled. Why, in those days it was never possible for a family to be so organized as to have a double head. There could be but one diploma in a family and that belonged to the head of the house. To-day a college degree may belong to the other portion of the family and the head of it may be entirely without one. That is one of the changes. There were some things in those days that used to abound here. They may have continued to the present time, but there is one of them that impressed itself on my mind. At that time I inveighed against it. I never believed in it. Oh, that retiring bell! Many a time it fell on my unwilling ears and drove me away from these hospitable doors. But when in later years I have sought to reason against so many rules, Mrs. Hyde reminds me that had it not been for that retiring bell my constant appearance here might not have been crowned with success.

And now one thing more I wish to say. Professor Tyler, whom I have learned to revere because he was my teacher and because I have known him in all these succeeding years, is so wise that his wisdom must not be questioned, but I would say in addition to his advice to these young women to go South, "Go West, go South, if you will, but before you go please take a little advice of some of the young men who are graduating at this other institution. Don't go West wholesale unless they are willing to go too."

After all there is nothing that has come nearer to the graduates of Mt. Holyoke Seminary, nothing is more entwined with their lives, than the American Board, and I take great pleasure in presenting to you as the next speaker Rev. Dr. N. G. Clark.

Dr. CLARK.—I am very glad of such an introduction. I think it is very true that the American Board has had a large place in the sympathies of this institution, and when we point to fifty-six or more of its graduates now connected with the Board—one-fifth of all the women connected with our Board—it gives emphasis to your remarks, sir. I have been asking myself, however, what is the real secret of the power here. We hear of the influence of this seminary. We rejoice in it. And I thought as I heard this hymn sung, "O, born of faith, O, nursed in prayer," that there needed to be added one more exclamation to give the secret, O, consecrated to Christ! That I think is the secret of the power of this institution. It is that which has made it what it is, in its culture, in its type of character, in its influence round the world. And how came this special consecration? It was born, and nurtured by the Holy Spirit, in the heart of Mary Lyon. It was her consecration, her faith in God, that enabled her to lay hold not of mere human but of divine power, which she thus wrought into this institution and into the character and lives of its pupils. It was that faith that laid hold on the power of Him with whom is all power in heaven and on earth. And the spirit of Mary Lyon perpetuated in the instruction of this institution, in its silent hour, in all its manifold improvements by which Christian culture has been enlarged, that is the first element in securing this consecration to Christ. The trustees, and above all the teachers, have been consecrated to these sacred memories and traditions.

As a second influence comes in here the fact that the women who have come up to this institution have been largely Christian women. I never have known of an institution where so many young women were Christian to start with. Many came with Christian purpose. That has been developed here by the influence of the institution. The purpose to make their lives tell brought them here. Here they have been trained as nowhere else could they have been, and the institution having the best material to work upon has left its impression.

The third element, I am glad to say, has come from the foreign field. The letters that have come from consecrated women in every part of the globe, Africa, India, Japan, have all told on the Christian life and character of the young women here. How much Miss Fiske did for the cause of Christ in this institution! Perhaps more here through her example than she was enabled to do in Persia. I am profoundly grateful for this missionary correspondence, bringing home to the hearts of the pupils here the Christian work that is going on in the foreign field.

The fourth element has been this: the answers to prayer in every part of the world for a special blessing on Mt. Holyoke Seminary. "Nursed in prayer" not only here but by the prayers of the Christian church, by the prayers of graduates in all parts of the world. Thus there has been a volume ascending to God that has brought down blessings here as nowhere else. Let us recognize gratefully the divine blessing in answering the prayers of his people.

Thus we have a consecrated institution from first to last, and that has been the supreme thought. I know of no wiser sentence than that of Mary Lyon: "Be willing to go where no one else will go; to do what no one else will do." There is the practical spirit of consecration to Christ. Let this spirit prevail, to go where no one else will go,—to the heart of Japan, to China, down South among the lowly there, and we shall see great results. I would like to modify the advice to these young women to go West and to go South. I would say go round the world. I would like to add to it: Do not be satisfied with this country. This is the grandest country under heaven to be developed from. But the Lord lays on you, graduates of this school, the work of building up the kingdom of God the world over. Nothing less than that be your ambition, young women; no less than that the aim and purpose of this seminary. Less than that will be false to the spirit of Mary Lyon, to your opportunity, to your duty.

And that brings me to this one thought. I ask you Christian women to take advantage with us of this great tidal wave of missionary spirit which comes now as never before in the history of the Christian church. It came when all things were ready, when this country had been developed to be a power for the gospel as no other country, when means of entrance were open, when the world was open everywhere to Christian efforts, when the millions of Japan were begging for Christian teachers, when the heart of Africa, the Dark Continent, was open, when China was ready for us. When all these were ready this great tidal wave of missionary effort began, starting at Cambridge and Oxford, largely through the labors of Mr. Moody, spreading up to Edinboro', thence to Mt. Hermon, thence to our institutions of learning, till to-day over three thousand young men and women stand pledged to missionary work, the most marked feature of the Christian church. And now I call on you of Mt. Holyoke for your part in it. So may this institution be, in the latter days as in the first, one of the grandest agencies for promoting the kingdom of God upon the earth.

MR. HYDE.—When I went to Boston some twenty years ago, to enter upon the practice of my profession, I found there a man in the front rank, who was sought for to be retained in every important case that came into our courts. Again and again in later days have I wished that he was still there—for he left the profession—that I might secure him to assist me in some difficult case. Had he remained a few of you might have heard of him, but his name certainly would not have gone round and round the world as it has since. Giving up the law among us, he came to South Hadley with his wife and studied the workings of this institution, and, as a result to-day, the young women of America are blessing the memory of Mr. and Mrs. Durant. And one of the matters of rejoicing to-day is that one of the children of Mt. Holyoke has entered upon so large a career of success that she calls on us to put forth our best efforts to keep alongside of her. But the same cause that is being promoted here is being promoted there, and it gives me great pleasure to introduce to you the president of Wellesley College, Miss Freeman.

MISS FREEMAN.—*Dear Graduates of Mt. Holyoke Seminary:* Wellesley makes me to-day her happy messenger to bring to you the love and the greeting of your daughter Wellesley. Our president could not have said anything to make her daughter Wellesley so glad and so grateful as this which he has said of those two great souls, who, in the inspiration of this seminary, made it possible for us to come with our blessing to you to-day. I do not think it is customary for daughters to sit down calmly in the face of their mothers and tell them how they love them, in public. But when the queen mother has been queen for fifty years, and when she comes to her golden wedding and her coronation, then the daughters must be permitted to have their say, and so your youngest daughter comes to you to bless you that she is alive and that you are alive; to tell you how glad we are that you are so much alive, and that you make it possible for us to live in the light of your presence. I cannot come to you with Wellesley's greeting and not tell you in just a word, why it is that every daughter and teacher of Wellesley, yes, and I may say of other schools, blesses you and loves you and prays for your peace. It is because of certain things that you have done for us that make it possible for us to live the life God gives us to live. I remember one October night when the leaves were falling on these hills, when I stood for the first time down by that marble where are inscribed the best words, I think, that woman ever said: "I know of nothing that I am afraid of but that I may not know my whole duty, or may fail to do it." Those words have been the inspiration of thousands of women's hearts who bless your brave and tender-hearted leader and queen. You have made it possible for us women to believe as we never could have believed before, that whatever God gives to woman to do she can do, and that there is nothing, nothing, to be afraid of in all the world, but that we shall not claim and keep the promise that your Mary Lyon illustrated in her life. You have done what no other women have done in overcoming all obstacles, as to-day illustrates. If it were possible to drown enthusiasm—as it is to drown voices—then and only then could you fail on this anniversary day to illustrate how no danger, no difficulties, no trouble, ever stood against the work Mary Lyon did or tried to do. We feel this as we are drawn together in spite of the rain, so that we are gladder of the rain than of the sunshine. You have taught us to be brave, generous, and you have taught us the lesson that most of all the citizens of this land need to learn to-day, that after all our life does not consist in the things we possess, not indeed in what we know, not in what we can do, but in what we can be, and we bless you for it. We bless you in the name of that grand, great soul, that looking on you here gave Wellesley to the world. We bless you in her name who prays with you here to-day. We bless you in the name of all the teachers and girls that you have sent us to make us better, and in the name of all the Wellesley girls that go to meet you round the world. We are glad and grateful, and we pledge you our devotion and our loyalty. I come to tell you that Wellesley women, if they deserve the name of your friends, will follow you round the world; that your empire and ours shall be greater than the Queen's, the Queen of Britain and of India; that you and we together shall, with our prayer and our work and our hope and our faith and our life, build on the foundations which Christ and Mary Lyon laid here on these hills.

In Wellesley chapel, where day by day our daughters are brought together, there is a word that faces them forever that we learned of you: "Not to be ministered unto, but to minister." And on one side we have written the words that Mr. Durant left for us: "God so loved the world that He sent his Son," and on the other side: "Here am I; send me." This we bring as our greeting and our pledge. And we pray that peace may be within your walls and prosperity within your palaces.

MR. HYDE.—There is in my family a daily discussion as to whether, twenty-five years ago, Amherst or Mt. Holyoke furnished the better education. We have some children studying Latin, and when they find a difficult passage they don't come to me for assistance, for the reason, they say, that my wife is a better scholar than I am. And the only way that I have been able to preserve the reputation of my college is to say that the pupils were not equal in the start. When I was invited to preside here we had a household-conference, and I was asked who would be the speakers, and I read over the list that had been sent me, and among others was the name of Miss Freeman. When that was learned I was told in my family conference that I might prepare myself and do the best I could, but she would certainly surpass me: the words of the woman are wise above that of the man.

I have now the pleasure of introducing the Rev. Mr. Harding of Longmeadow.

REV. MR. HARDING.—It has been suggested that as a pastor of somewhat long continuance [thirty-seven years] in one of the old churches of the Connecticut valley and representative of many others, I should say a few words respecting the work of this institution and its value at home and abroad. Let me begin with boasting a little of the civilization of this valley. Taking it all in all, tracing it from the head-waters of the river to the Sound, including its diffused intelligence, its numerous and various beneficent institutions, its colleges, Dartmouth, Amherst, Smith, Mt. Holyoke (only too modest to assume the name), Trinity, Wesleyan; its academies and auxiliary schools too numerous to mention; its asylums for the manifold relief of human suffering; its smiling villages, cultured and restful homes; its expanding cities and thriving manufactures;—I venture to say that this Connecticut valley civilization has not its counterpart for the same extent of territory, and viewed in the sum total of its desirable characteristics, the world over. I proceed to say that from the outset, in the building of this remarkable civilization, the women were equal to the men. They have always wrought hand in hand with the men, and especially as queens and princesses of the Christian home. This is the true unit of this civilization, even before the church, the school, or the town-meeting. They were of the type described by the preacher in the book of Ecclesiastes: "They laid their hands to the spindle, and their hands held the distaff; they stretched out their hands to the poor; they looked well to the ways of their households, and they ate not the bread of idleness; they opened their mouths with wisdom, and in their tongues was the law of kindness. The hearts of their husbands did safely trust in them: their children rise up and call them blessed." Such women as Mary Pynchon, Jerusha Edwards, Margaret Bliss, Sarah Williston, and in their true succession, Mary Lyon. "Give them of the fruit of their hands; and let their works praise them in the gates." I proceed further to say that if the women were equal from the outset to the men, since Mary Lyon's day they have been superior to the men, at least in the average make-up of our rural towns.

After singing one verse of "All hail the power of Jesus' name," Mr. Hyde introduced Miss Evans of Painesville.

MISS EVANS.—*Mr. President:* This is a great thing to ask of a woman, to speak in such a place as this, and were it not that I have always been taught obedience at Mt. Holyoke I never, never, never could do it.

It is not enough to say that Miss Lyon gave a great impulse to the higher education of women. She had a direct and personal influence in the establishment of other Mt. Holyoke Seminaries. Her interest in the great and growing West was shared by Miss Grant and resulted in sending forth teachers from Derry and Ipswich, and later from Mt. Holyoke, to such places as Granville and Willoughby in Ohio, and to other and more western states. Some of these schools have ceased to be connected with Mt. Holyoke; some are merged in other schools, while two or three have kept up their Holyoke connection, have celebrated their twenty-fifth anniversaries, and have their hundreds of graduates in this and other lands. These have been known as "the kindred schools," the Western Seminary at Oxford and the Lake Erie Seminary at Painesville, both in Ohio, and, though somewhat later in birth, the Michigan Seminary at Kalamazoo.

But we are not to think of ourselves as the first or only Holyoke schools. The recently published history of Mt. Holyoke Seminary gives the proper order as to the time of establishment, and also shows that the Holyoke connection is wider than the West: Oroomiah in Persia, 1845; Willoughby, O., 1847, out of which Lake Erie Seminary was formed, ten years later; the Western at Oxford, 1855; the seminary in Marsovan, Turkey, 1864; Mills College and Seminary in California, 1865; Michigan Seminary, 1867; the school in Bitlis, Turkey, 1868; Huguenot Seminary in South Africa, 1874; and to these should be added the Constantinople Home School, the Spanish Mt. Holyoke in Northern Spain, Mt. Hermon Seminary for colored girls in Mississippi, and many another school of Holyoke aim and spirit, presided over by Holyoke graduates.

But, name or number them as we may, it is interesting to trace in their history the working out of those principles of equality and independence and self-denial for Christ's sake which have made them truly Holyoke and truly kindred schools. How interesting to see the domestic work system transplanted entire into South Africa, where the colonial traditions of housework and so-called menial service must have been quite in the opposite direction. While we, in America, were beginning to doubt whether girls could mop floors and keep up some other domestic duties, these Huguenot daughters were cheerfully laying their hands to the broom, and even to the mop handle.

Some of our best and largest gifts have come to us in the line of our Holyoke principles. A gentleman, visiting Michigan Seminary, who was not greatly moved even by its religious aim, did view with satisfaction the family life and the domestic work, and quietly determined that his money, to the extent of forty thousand dollars, should go to such a school. The seminary at Oxford, Holyoke of the Holyokes, mother of missionaries, school of faith and prayer, where they have come through fiery trials without even the smell of fire on their garments, where they have wrought righteousness and obtained promises—what makes tender a hundred hearts all round the world at the very names of Miss Peabody and Miss Jessup? There, the missionary spirit of Miss Lyon is embodied in a wonderful way. A trustee of that school, whose recent death has made a breach not soon to be filled, said, when told of one of its missionary daughters, who had paid for her board and tuition by extra domestic work: "We must help such girls." And he did help by the establishment of a fund of ten thousand dollars for their aid, besides other generous gifts. We, at Painesville, have seen one noble giver, the Hon. Reuben Hitchcock, now gone to his reward, giving, year by year, without ostentation, and as needs arose, one thousand—ten thousand dollars, to keep the board and tuition at the lowest rate consistent with justice, till at last his gifts had exceeded sixty thousand dollars, and his honored name remains with us in the Hitchcock Fund of twenty-five thousand dollars for the aid of just such students as Miss Lyon desired to train for Christian service. And what inspired a woman's heart—she is here with us to-day—to set aside, while she lived, fifty thousand dollars for the endowment of the "Mark Hopkins chair of Mental and Moral Philosophy" in Mills College, but the earnest purpose to do for California through that school what Mt. Holyoke does for the East? So true is it that those who stand for the great principles which the work of Miss Lyon represented, shall see their triumph, sooner or later, in the educational movements of the world.

Not that we possess a monopoly of these everlasting principles. It would be as false as it would be foolish to claim for ourselves that we, more than all other schools, stand for thoroughness and faithfulness and sympathy with all broad and generous work for Christ and humanity. How could we, at Painesville, say or think it, so near our neighbor Oberlin, or Rockford, a little farther west, both having so much in common with Holyoke spirit and history? And you of the mother school would not say it, near colleges long past their semi-centennial, and seminaries like Abbot and Bradford and Wheaton telling over their years and their honors, and your young neighbors, Wellesley and Smith, girding themselves for their fifty years of labor and reward? No, it is not like Mary Lyon to think that Mt. Holyoke schools are, alone, favored of God, and a blessing to the world.

What, then, have we, as kindred schools, to uphold as a special feature of our common work? With what highest aim of the higher education shall we enkindle our souls as we praise "the mother of us all," and rejoice in our heritage? It seems to me that one trust is ours by our Holyoke birth and lineage, and by the call of our times—to keep and cultivate, along with all possible enlargement in things intellectual, the home spirit which has made this place so dear to all who have studied here. "Who are these that fly as a cloud and as doves to their windows?" Who but those who have come *home?* And what but this loyal, loving spirit could keep up courage while these floods descend upon us? Who thinks of weariness or even of best bonnets and best gowns? And yet we are women, and for nothing less than *alma mater* and this home coming could we "take joyfully the spoiling of our goods."

"The right ordering of families is God's social science," said our revered, beloved, and now sainted teacher, Dr. Hopkins.

"To make a happy fireside clime
Is the true pathos and sublime
Of human life,"

says one of our poets. But how to make home and school one is a problem. There shines before me, as a light to guide and cheer, that picture of Miss Lyon with her writing desk in a corner of the domestic hall, beside the Rumford oven, conducting the seminary correspondence and superintending the bread-making for the family, great teacher, wise woman of affairs, mistress of the home, all in one. But how can we keep on in her footsteps? The college idea for women is in the air, and it is well. The home idea and the college idea are both needed in our educational plans. The problem is not to reconcile them as if they were adverse, but to adjust them in harmonious proportion. There never was a time in the history of our land when we needed to think more of the home, and we cannot afford to leave out of our school systems the training which the home idea implies. True, the family life of this seminary led to the making of many rules. Because we did our own ironing, and because the principles of good housekeeping forbade it, we were not to set our hot irons on the ironing-board; and because we were responsible for knowing and doing our duty, we were to tell whether or not we had burned that ironing-board cover. And so the rules multiplied till, to some, the pendulum seemed to swing to the furthest point in the arc. Then it began to swing back towards the middle, and it is still swinging towards that golden mean between the extreme of over carefulness and morbid conscientiousness and the extreme of carelessness and "wicked waste that makes woful want." The home idea has been the blessing and glory of Mt. Holyoke, but, blessed and God-given as it is, it must not become narrowing. We may be so busy with our sweeping and dusting and setting things to rights that we may not take heed of what the world wants of us, and so the world—not the wicked world, but the great world that God so loved—may not wait for us, but go elsewhere for help. But, then, the great world does not always know what it is asking for. When it asks of us women, at once college trained and home trained, it should not forget what a problem it sets before us, to keep the family life, with its complication of rules, with its extra time for housework, with its needful watch and ward, and harmonize with it the broader college idea of freedom from rules and freedom in choice of studies and additional time for the more exacting and absorbing studies of the college course. How can we study calculus and set tables, and if we must give up one or the other, which shall we not do?

But is the problem beyond us? Are we not, rather, summoned to study it in faith and prayer, as Mt. Holyoke enters on its second fifty years? Faith and prayer must be first as we reckon up our helps to its right solution. Wisdom is ours for the asking, and let us "ask in faith, nothing wavering." And in the lower sphere, let us rely on time—this problem is not to be solved in a day—on patience and a hearty co-operation on the part of trustees, teachers, and alumnæ. It must not be forgotten that women have hearts as well as heads to be trained and bodies to be cared for. Some burdens of dress must be laid aside that they may rise to their opportunities in these days. We must provide for carrying out the home idea in their training in proper buildings, and besides time and patience and wisdom we need money. While every one is thinking of scientific buildings for Mt. Holyoke and enlargements in the line of study, may I be pardoned for bringing out my hobby? It is to come up out of the basement into a dining hall which shall stand four square to all the breezes and the sunshine of heaven and which shall educate by its fitness and beauty all who gather within it three times each day. Even the kitchen should be the best and brightest that could be built. So must the home be considered while the college grows, and so shall we be true to the Mary Lyon ideal of training the whole woman in wholeness of body, soul, and spirit.

The problem is before us for our study. It grows greater to me as I speak of it. But then, I was never good in algebra. I have been speaking my thanks to my teacher, now in attendance upon this jubilee, for her laborious and faithful efforts in bringing me safely through this part of my course of study. She taught me to state a problem, to indicate the factors in it and the method of solving it. But, not always did I succeed in the solution. I fear that, as in the old, dull days, so now, I can only state and leave it. It is for us of the kindred schools, as for you in this mother school, to be loyal to the idea of Mary Lyon as she was loyal to Christ, and so shall we study our problem, and so, God helping, we shall solve it.

MR. HYDE.—If the whole history of the fifty years closing were to be accurately written and the lives of all those who are gathered here to-day were also to be written, we should be surprised to find how the history of every land and the progress of other people were somehow touched by the experience of the seminary. But write that history as we may and speak of the experience of those who are here, and of those who would be glad to be here if they might, if there were left out the history of Turkey there would be left a large blank which could not be filled. Constantinople has been, since the days of written history, one of the great central points, and we have with us to-day a gentleman from that city, who can tell us not only of life there but of the inspiration he has received in his life from Mt. Holyoke Seminary. I take pleasure in presenting Professor Millingen, of Robert College.

MR. MILLINGEN.—*Ladies and Gentlemen:* I am a son-in-law of Mt. Holyoke Seminary. There are a great many of them, I am happy to say. Not many weeks ago I was down at Fisk University and was asked to give some account of the grand work in Constantinople. In doing so I spoke, of course, of the young ladies' home at Scutari, when one of my colored hearers suddenly asked: "What do the Home graduates do?" I was taken a little aback for the moment, but replied in an instant: "They marry." It seemed to them exceedingly funny, but it may be said of Mt. Holyoke graduates also, "they marry." Out of the 1,992 graduates of this seminary 1,787 of them have married, and I want to-day to present the tribute of our gratitude to our revered mother-in-law for the 1,787 bright and happy homes that she has enabled her daughters to form. I know that sons-in-law have not the reputation of being the most grateful race upon this earth; that it is an exceptional virtue for a son-in-law to cherish much affection for his mother-in-law. Not long ago a distinguished divine of this country received the honor of being made president of one of your universities. A pastor of that city called to offer congratulations, and in the course of the conversation the president was asked where he intended to spend his summer vacation. He replied in one of the hill towns of Connecticut. The pastor was amazed and asked: "Why do you spend your vacation in that little sleepy New England village? why not go with me to the Atlantic coast?" The president replied: "My wife's mother lives in that sleepy New England village, and as long as she lives I shall spend my summer vacations there." The pastor was so impressed that he sat down and wrote a sermon on the virtue of filial devotion, and in the course of it he referred to this instance and spoke of it as a remarkable example which led a distinguished divine to spend his summer vacation in a sleepy New England village for the sake of his mother, and she his mother-in-law. But I think it all turns upon the daughters whether the sons-in-law are filial or not, and no one who is a son-in-law of Mt. Holyoke Seminary can fail to cherish the most filial devotion for his mother-in-law. I had to read two lives of Mary Lyon before I received the slightest favor or encouragement, and it was only after I had given proof of having a disposition to revere my mother-in-law that I was accepted.

There is one other duty that I wish to discharge besides the one I have just performed, and that is to thank Mt. Holyoke for the beautiful daughters she has sent to do missionary work in Turkey. I am glad to greet several of them here this afternoon. I wish to say to Mt. Holyoke that her daughters have left a name and done a work in that land which have made her own name dear and beloved. The thought in Mary Lyon's mind from which this institution sprung has always seemed to me one of the most beautiful that could be held in mind. Your valley is beautiful, your residence is beautiful; I do not wonder that yon river lingers on its way to the sea; but the idea that she put into this institution was that this is no beauty compared with the beauty that excelleth. I love almost everything about that thought. And what particularly strikes me is the penetration with which she recognized wherein lies one of the great social forces of the world. It is not so much in other parts of her idea that she seems to me to stand so high and to deserve to be so memorable, as in being the discoverer of a new force to push the world forward toward all that is good. We revere the names of such men as Luther, who dwelt upon the rights of individual conscience; we revere the name of the man who discovered the value of the child's mind and who brought the attention of the church to the cultivation of the child's mind in Sunday-school work, as one of the great factors for the improvement and enlightenment of mankind, but along with them is to be placed Mary Lyon for discovering the power of woman to bless the world. Her idea in regard to female education was not to make women better, women wiser, women freer from restrictions, but to bring woman alongside of the powers that were blessing the world. It is from that point of view that she seems to me to deserve the honor and the praise which we are gathered to give her this day.

There is one other thought. Is this work to be perpetuated? The generation that saw Mary Lyon is almost gone. It will soon pass away, and the generation that followed is going. It is getting smaller and smaller, and in the midst of these vanishing scenes the question naturally occurs, how about the perpetuity of the influence of this institution? In Constantinople there is an aqueduct that spans the valley between two of the seven hills on which the city stands. It was built in the fourth century of our era, and from that century to the present hour there has flowed from reservoirs of water in the distant forest a stream to quench the thirst of the multitudes who dwell in that great metropolis. Fifteen hundred years have passed since that aqueduct was reared, but still its work of beneficence has gone on, blessing generation after generation. And, friends, the spiritual forces which good men and good women organize in this world are not weaker than the material forces that men are using for the world's good. Just as that aqueduct has been blessing that city for a millennium and a half, so the influence flowing from this institution will go on after this generation and the next and the next shall have all passed away. Let us then work as those who are working for that which shall endure.

MR. HYDE.—Among the memories that come back to this day are the memories of the many teachers whom you have loved in the past and whose presence you love still, and these exercises would be incomplete were you not to hear from one of the loving teachers of Mt. Holyoke. I therefore have the pleasure of presenting to you Miss Edwards.

MISS EDWARDS.—*Good Friends,—Dear Friends!* how shall I voice the feelings of *alma mater* to day? Twenty-five years ago the sight of the procession of graduates and the experiences of anniversary week kindled my enthusiasm, and I said: "Let me live to see the fiftieth anniversary." The wish of my heart has been granted, and to-day I am like a school girl again.

When I assisted in gathering statistics about the alumnæ twenty-five years ago, the work seemed to me dry and uninteresting; but now the names before us stand for living realities. There is not one of all the six thousand that has not been gone over and over again, till we can almost say, "We have found them all." Many are here unseen,—

"Not dead, not sleeping, not even gone,
But present still."

And Mary Lyon, too, I believe is in our assembly to-day.

Turning now to the future I cannot help a feeling of sadness at the thought of changes that must come, important and desirable as they will be. But as there never was a time in the past when we were willing to stand still, so let us bravely press on; let our thoughts take hold on eternity in that straight line that turns neither to the right nor the left but goes on forever.

> "Then gin I thinke on that which nature sayd
>   Of that same time when no more change shall be,
> But stedfast rest of all things, firmly stayed
>   Upon the pillars of eternity.
> O thou God of Sabaoth hight,
> Grant me that Sabbath sight!"

MR. HYDE.—The first work that Mary Lyon ever did which tended to make her name a household word was the soliciting of money for Mt. Holyoke Seminary. And one of the alumnæ has made up her mind that, unless some of you shall give what she wants without it, her name shall be a household word also, until the endowment shall be what it needs to be. If any of you have a feeling that you do not desire her acquaintance and wish her not to invade your homes or counting-rooms, you would better send her a check early next week, for I assure you that if you are blessed with anything like a competence you will have a smaller bank account after a visit from her. I have the pleasure of introducing Mrs. Smith of Detroit, Mich., President of the Alumnæ Association.

MRS. SMITH.—It has been said that fifty years ago two young women entered upon their different courses of life. A little more than fifty years ago two powerful forces entered into the world. During the same years that Mary Lyon was going up and down this state inspiring the people to believe in her and her enterprise, the founder of the electric telegraph was going up and down England, France, and this country, endeavoring to secure means by which his invention should be made known. He besieged Congress till the money came. In the same year that the electric telegraph flashed over the line its first message: "What hath God wrought!" in that very year Mt. Holyoke Seminary was founded with the motto: "That our daughters may be as corner-stones polished after the similitude of a palace." Those forces have worked side by side. We all know that the telegraph has revolutionized the world. Life is truer and better for it. The life of the humblest peasant on Alpine heights is brighter and better and stronger for what Morse did. But that other force, Mt. Holyoke Seminary, working along the channels of human life, touching on human purpose, has wrought a wider revolution, and is to-day the more signal power of the two. The revolution that has been wrought by the development of the power of woman is felt, not only in America, but in all the nations of the wide world. It started with the giving of the ten-cent subscriptions to Mary Lyon, and the millions in the harems of Turkey and the women in the islands of the sea are feeling the influence. But there is a great difference in one respect between these two forces. There have been millions and millions of money put into the electric telegraph. It never would have been the power it is but for that first grant which Congress gave and for that which men have freely put into it since. They say they cannot live without it. But society cannot live and be a power without the influence of such an institution as this. The great problem of the world is salvation from sin, and the ages are solving it, but woman is the prime factor in the solution. Woman is the only agency that shall reach great numbers of humanity with the gospel of Jesus Christ. To-day there is need that millions shall be put into educational institutions, and millions are being put into them, but they have not yet been put into Mt. Holyoke Seminary. We have been too modest, too economical, too self-denying, in some respects. But to-day, because of its widespread religious power for the honor of Jesus Christ, I say it reverently, in order that this institution may equal any institution in the land for men or for women, let it have an endowment that is enough,—not a paltry hundred thousand dollars. Five hundred thousand may do for a few years; presently a million will be needed, and we must have it. There is enough in the world. Millionaires are no longer solitaire jewels. Boston alone has fifteen women millionaires in their own right. Every one of you must now be agents to bring in this money. It will not do to go forth with the understanding that we are going to be satisfied with any small sum. If you honor your *alma mater*, if you honor the cause of Christ, if you know what has been wrought through this institution, use your utmost endeavors to turn into the channels of this institution the money that is to be had. Mr. Moody walks into Boston and comes out with fifty, sixty, seventy, a hundred thousand dollars. That is what you and I must do. It is an insult to go to rich men and women and ask for small sums. They want to be rated with those people who give large sums. We are glad of the ten-cent subscriptions and the dollar subscriptions. They come many times as consecrated gifts and we thank God for them, but the time has come to set the wheel rolling for large sums for this institution. Do you know a rich man anywhere? Go and ask him for money for this school. Do not wait. There is no place left for laggards. Do it right away. This institution should be made to stand at the forefront of all women's colleges in this wide land. Let it be the chiefest star of honor as it was the first that went before and led the way.

MR. HYDE.—When Dr. Hitchcock handed me the list of speakers I asked him how I should arrange them. "You may put the women in anywhere," he said, "and I will answer for the result." You see that he was justified.

Mr. Hyde then read the following letter from President Seelye of Smith College:—

"It is with sincere regret that I find myself unable to accept your invitation to attend the semi-centennial exercises at Mt. Holyoke Seminary. I should like at least to testify to the obligation which our higher schools for women are under to Mary Lyon and to the institution which she founded. Most of them owe their very existence to

Mt. Holyoke Seminary; all of them are unspeakably indebted to the work which it has accomplished during the past fifty years in providing better and more abundant material for their work; in educating so many accomplished and self-sacrificing teachers; and in giving so clear and forcible expression to the truth that intelligence is as valuable in a woman's mind as it is in a man's, and is as capable and as worthy of the highest cultivation. I congratulate you on what the seminary has been, on what it is, on what it is to be. Rich as it is in the precious heritage of the past, in the material and intellectual resources of the present, I am sure the coming years have a grander work for it to accomplish."

MR. HYDE.—That you may not feel over proud of what has been accomplished here I do not forget that in my college days I was instructed to revere the story of Homer and that the occasion of that story was the Grecian maiden Helen, I therefore ask our friend, the Greek professor at Smith College, to give us in any language he pleases his opinion of the difference between the Hellenic period and that of to-day.

PROF. H. M. TYLER.—I thoroughly sympathize with your disappointment that our president is not here to-day. Some years since I was asked to represent him in a neighboring church where he was expected to supply the pulpit. I presented myself before the committee, and the chairman of the committee said, "Did you say, sir, that the president is ill?" I said, "Yes." "And that he sent you to take his place?" I answered, "Yes." "Well," was the reply, "our people will be very much disappointed." I can only say, however, that as I have been sitting here this afternoon, waiting my hour to come, that I have been as sorry as you.

When I started out to take my journey hither this morning, I found that my hat had suddenly grown a little too large for me; that some one had gone off with my hat and left his with me. I felt it was rather ominous for the proceedings of the day that I was to attempt to put myself into a heavier man's place and that it would be too much for me to draw an Odysseus' bow which was too great for my power.

This morning we were told that we were all children of Mt. Holyoke Seminary, but Miss Freeman suggests that she brings the greeting of the "youngest daughter." How is it with Smith then? Are we twins? At all events it gives me great pleasure to bring greetings from the daughter or sister across the river. The chairman has introduced me with a suggestion of Greek. I have been thinking this morning, as I sat listening to the orator of the morning—for whom I have the greatest respect—that with all the Latin which he brought before you, he certainly ought to have brought in a little Greek. Perhaps therefore I may be permitted to add a suggestion, even if it introduce a little Greek, that came into my mind. I hope that I may be able to make the quotation, a hope that is somewhat encouraged from the fact that I have for several hours to-day worn the hat of the Greek professor of Amherst College. Somewhere among the fragments which are left to us from Simonides of Ceos, there is one written on a monument whereon a sculptured lion rested above the tomb of a man whose name was Leon. And this inscription was wrought on it:—

Θηρῶν μὲν κάρτιστος ἐγώ, θνατῶν δ', ὃν ἐγὼ νῦν
φρουρῶ, τῷδε τάφῳ λαΐνῳ ἐμβεβαώς·
ἀλλ' εἰ μὴ θυμόν γε Λέων ἐμόν, οὔνομά τ' εἶχεν,
οὐκ ἂν ἐγὼ τύμβῳ τῷδ' ἐπέθηκα πόδας.

"I am the strongest of beasts, and I guard the strongest of mortals. If Leon had been merely my name and not my spirit I never should have stood here above this sepulcher of stone." And so I think if Mary Lyon had had only the name but not the heart which her name suggested we should not have been here to celebrate her remembrance to-day.

The more I study the problems of the present time the more I am convinced that in order to do good to men you must educate them. If you preach to a man you must teach him; you must educate him in the commands of God. If you bring charity to a man, if you give five or ten dollars a day to a man who has been used to earn but fifty cents or a dollar, you give him nothing if you leave him a fifty cents or a dollar man. It is only the introduction to spiritual and moral resources which makes men rich. Poverty consists not merely in the lack of material resources. And assuredly if there is any great movement in modern times it is this movement with which woman has been so superlatively connected, this movement which has been for the enlarged education and uplifting of the human race prominently through woman's agency. And if there is any institution upon the face of the broad earth which has been connected in various avenues with this grand movement of progress in modern times it is this institution of Mt. Holyoke, carrying out the spirit which was in Mary Lyon. I cannot stop, and need not if I could, to add fine moral remarks this afternoon. Among all the exercises to-day I have been particularly moved and delighted with the singing that we listened to this morning. It seemed to me there was a sound of peculiar triumph in the songs as they went upward from the choir. I can only say in my greeting from Smith College that I trust after fifty years the students of Smith College may have as good reason to triumph as have the students of Mt. Holyoke Seminary to-day, and that they may have as sweet voices, as well trained and as well educated for song as those we have listened to to-day. And may the triumph which belongs to us partake, as much as God may grant to us to make it partake, of that same spirit of consecration and faith and zeal which breathed in Mary Lyon and has made itself felt here for the blessing of American homes, the blessing of American institutions, and the blessing of lives throughout the world.

Numerous appreciative letters were received containing congratulations and good wishes. The following extracts will serve as samples of the warm expressions regarding the work thus far accomplished by the seminary:—

"All mankind are your debtors. Mary Lyon and her associates and successors have lifted our race, by quickening its intellect and converting its heart. In homes, in churches, and in Christian and benevolent institutions,—in mission stations in heathen lands, as well as in our own land, her spirit still lives whose only fear it was that she might not know her whole duty, or that she might fail to do it."

"For the noble work which the seminary has done in training enlightened, consecrated women, it deserves and has the love and reverence of the entire nation."

"Please accept my most hearty congratulations on the favoring providences that have guided and sustained the seminary through its first half century, on the already abundant fulfillment of the noble purposes of its founder, and on the consequent promise of yet larger usefulness in future years. There must be a great multitude consciously debtors to the seminary whose hearts will keep the festival of this half century, not only in our own land, but in all the lands to which our American churches have carried the gospel of Jesus Christ. And there must be a still larger number of unconscious debtors to Miss Lyon and her associates through the stimulus that the seminary has given to the Christian education of young women.

"I rejoice to think that when a noble Christian life passes beyond our sight to the immortality of heaven, it may leave behind an institution imbued with its spirit, and that the earthly institution may maintain, even here, an immortality parallel with that to which its founder has passed. So it is with Miss Lyon—and with the institution that she founded. She lives—and the seminary lives—both, I trust, advancing continually in the service and in the joy of our Lord."

MR. HYDE.—Two hours ago recollection was the duty of the hour. The hours have passed and we turn from the fifty years that have gone and look toward the fifty years to come. May they be no less full of blessing and of beneficence. May they go out to all the world with all the influence of the years just closing. As we turn to that future I would suggest that Miss Blanchard, the worthy successor of Miss Lyon, step forward, and that, with full utterance of heart-felt gratitude, we all join in singing "Home, Sweet Home."

Mr. Hyde led Miss Blanchard to the front of the platform; the congregation rose and sang "Home, Sweet Home."

The benediction was pronounced by President Seelye.

AFTERWARD.

MANY left at the close of the exercises in the tent, others remained for the senior reception in the evening; while a goodly number were led by "the clear shining after rain" to defer their departure on Friday that they might visit old haunts as they could not during the storm; a few who had no other alternative had resolutely braved the tempest on Thursday to gratify the desire once more to visit the monument under the trees, or to stand again on the footbridge over the dam. Never were the grounds more attractive nor the walks or drives in Goodnow Park and elsewhere more inviting than on the "perfect days" that followed. Mrs. Eaton was right when she said, "The white-haired scholars will seek out Mr. Condit's grave this week as well as Miss Lyon's." Some lingered until after the Sabbath and went once more to worship in the village church, where Dr. Love ministers in the place of Mr. Condit and his successors. These guests and all resident alumnæ were invited, by a notice in church, to gather in the seminary parlors at three o'clock, and about seventy assembled. Among them were the three daughters of Miss Lyon's early co-laborer, Mr. Hawks, who were present at the laying of the corner-stone, who helped get the first dinner when the seminary opened, and who graduated together in 1842. One of them was married in the seminary hall, Thanksgiving evening, 1850.

The meeting was described as a "fitting close of a blessed week." After the recitation of responsive passages, Mrs. Gulliver asked for single texts, or promises, or prayers of thanksgiving in "memory of Thy great goodness." The request called forth an outpouring of tender reminiscences, grateful recognition, and earnest desires for the future of the seminary. A suggestion from

Miss Ward was followed by an affectionate remembrance of Miss Jessup, Miss Ellis, and all alumnæ laid aside by suffering. A daughter mentioned gratefully the indebtedness of those whose mothers had been Holyoke students. A recent graduate, impressed by the beautiful faces among the older alumnæ, reminded her classmates and others how they might honor *alma mater* by making their own lives beautiful. Miss Edwards presented Mrs. Eaton's request for the appointment of a weekly concert of prayer for all the alumnæ, and it was proposed to give wider notice of the hour already observed by many, at eight, Saturday evening. In this connection Miss Edwards read the following from an editorial in the Springfield *Union* of June 24 :—

There are thousands of families in New England, and people all over the country and the world, who consider themselves related to Mt. Holyoke, because it is the *alma mater* of wives, mothers, sisters, daughters, cousins, or relatives even more remote, who have never ceased to love their seminary home. It is doubtful whether there is an institution of education in the world, which can focus to itself on such an occasion as this week's, so many loving thoughts and hallowed recollections from a field so wide. There is not a quarter of the globe where good women have not looked back to the old home this week and wished to be there, and we dare to believe that, in the unseen land, many saintly spirits of Mt. Holyoke alumnæ have joined in sending down their love and blessing to their *alma mater*.

Whether Mt. Holyoke should change its name from "seminary" to "college" is a matter of small importance compared with the question whether the institution shall change its character. It has done a peculiar and wonderful work in the fifty years of its existence and there is place for the same kind of work for fifty years to come. That sort of work is still needed and if the seminary should retain its present status it would never lack pupils. It is true that there is now a demand for a higher and broader education than that contemplated in the founding of the seminary, but there is also a demand for the same methods that have been pursued in the past. Mt. Holyoke Seminary should retain its old character, but it may do that and become a college, also. There is room for an advance upon new lines, and a college department might be added without detriment to the seminary department. The fact that Wellesley and Smith are both crowded seems to demand new facilities for collegiate education for women, and where could they be better supplied than at Mt. Holyoke? It is in order for the friends of the institution to propose this by the offer of grand endowments. Half a million dollars for woman's education could not be better applied than by giving it to the trustees of the seminary, for the purposes of advancement. Wealthy men and women who wish to execute their own wills can find no better investment for their money than Mt. Holyoke Seminary.

After other prayers, the hymn, "Blest be the tie that binds," was sung, and Miss Blanchard, who had given the greeting early in the week, now gave the God-speed at parting, in the words,—

"The Lord bless thee and keep thee;
"The Lord make his face shine upon thee and be gracious unto thee;
"The Lord lift up his countenance upon thee and give thee peace."

INDEX.

Address, Historical, Wm. S. Tyler, D. D., 3, 107; of Mrs. J. P. Cowles, 35; of welcome, Miss Blanchard, 31.
Addresses of Alumnæ, efforts to obtain, 5, 6.
After dinner speeches, N. G. Clark, D. D., 135; Miss Edwards, 145; Miss Evans, 139; Miss Freeman, 137; Rev. J. W. Harding, 139; H. D. Hyde, Esq., 133; Prof. Millingen, 143; Mrs. Moses Smith, 146; Prof. Tyler, 148.
Afterward, 151.
Alumnæ Association, Annual meeting of, 79; sketch of, 79.
Alumnæ, General Meeting of, 31.
Alumnæ at Work, Mrs. Chapin Pease, 38; Medical Work of, Dr. Peck, 44.
Anniversary and Graduating Exercises, 107.
At Home, Poem, Mrs. Angell Goodwin, 46.
Avery, Dea. Joseph, 65.

Baccalaureate Sermon, Thomas Laurie, D. D., 23.
Badges, for alumnæ and guests, 7.
Blake, Mrs., W. P. Ballard, To the Mothers, 57.
Blanchard, Miss, Address of Welcome, 31.
Branch Associations, reports from, 81.
Bruce, Harriet L., Hymn, 131.

Candee, Mrs., H. M. Hunt, The Stone of Scone, 71.
Carter, Mrs., H. M. Dodd, Reminiscences, 73.
Charter, grant of, commemorated, 3.
Choate, Hon. David, 63.
Clark, N. G., D. D., 135.
Clarke, Sarah A., Holyoke Alumnæ Associations, 79.
Class-meetings, 10.
Closing meeting of the week, 151.
Concert, weekly, of prayer, 79, 152.
Condit, Rev. Joseph D., 64.

Congregationalist, The, quoted, 12.
Corner-stone, 151; laying of commemorated, 5.
Cowles, Mrs. J. P., address of, 35.

Early Teachers, Mrs. Fiske Hart, 57.
Early Trustees, Mrs. Locke Stow, 63.
Eaton, Mrs., A. R. Webster, Our First Things at Mt. Holyoke Seminary, 51.
Edwards, Miss, 145.
Ellis, Miss, Letter from, 76.
Evans, Miss, 139.

First Things, Our, at Mt. Holyoke Seminary, Mrs. Webster Eaton, 51.
Freeman, Miss, 137.
Future of the Seminary, The, Mrs. Moses Smith, 101.

Gamwell, Mrs., S. A. DeWolf, Hymn, 100.
Goodwin, Mrs., H. J. Angell, Poem, 46.
Graduating Exercises, 130.
Gulliver, Mrs., H. M. French, Mary Lyon Fund, 4, 47.

Harding, Rev. J. W., 139.
Hart, Mrs., R. W. Fiske, Early Teachers, 57.
Hawks, Rev. Roswell, 64.
Historical Address, Wm. S. Tyler, D. D., 3, 107.
History of the Seminary, 3, 5, 8.
Hitchcock, Edward, D. D., 65.
Humphrey, Pres. Heman, 63.
Hyde, Henry D., Esq., 133.
Hymn, Harriet L. Bruce, 131.
Hymn, Mrs. DeWolf Gamwell, 100.
Hymn, Jubilee, S. F. Smith, D. D., 130.

Invitation Circular, 6.

Jessup, Miss, Letter from, 75.
Jubilee Hymn, S. F. Smith, D. D., 130.
Jubilee Week, 9.

Kirk, Edward N., D. D., 68.

INDEX. 155

Laurie, Thomas, D. D., Baccalaureate, 23.
Letters read, 147, 150 ; Miss Ellis, 76 ; Miss Jessup, 75 ; Miss Peabody, 77.

Mary Lyon Fund, proposed, 4 ; report upon, 47.
May, Julia H., A Reminiscence, 49.
Medical Work of the Alumnæ, Elizabeth L. Peck, M. D., 44.
Memorandum Catalogue, 5, 8.
Millingen, Prof., 143.
Missionary Association, The Mt. Holyoke, meeting of, 10.
Missionary Meeting, 15.
Morrill, Charlotte, Reminiscences, 87.

Old, The, and the New, Mrs. Spencer Severance, 92.

Park, Mrs., L. M. Carner, Poem, 32.
Parsons, Ellen C., Sacred Hours, 96.
Peabody, Miss, Letter from, 77.
Pease, Mrs., M. W. Chapin, 5 ; Alumnæ at Work, 38.
Peck, Elizabeth L., M. D., Medical Work of the Alumnæ, 44.
Poem, Mrs. Carner Park, 32.
Porter, Andrew W., 66.
Preparations, 3.
Presentation of diplomas, Pres. J. H. Seelye 130.

Reminiscence, A, Julia H. May, 49.
Reminiscences, Mrs. Dodd Carter, 73.
Reminiscences, Charlotte Morrill, 87.

Report. Mary Lyon Fund, Mrs. French Gulliver, 47.
Report, Treasurer of Alumnæ Association, 47, 81.
Reports, Branch Associations, 81.
Resolutions, 105.
Rice, Col. Austin, 65.

Sacred Hours, Ellen C. Parsons, 96.
Safford, Daniel, 67.
Science, Prominence given to, Miss Shattuck, 69.
Seelye, J. H., D. D., Presentation of diplomas, 130.
Seelye, L. Clark, D. D., 147.
Severance, Mrs., E. A. Spencer, The Old and the New, 92.
Shattuck, Miss, Prominence given to Science, 69.
Smith, Mrs., E. A. White, 146 ; The Future of the Seminary, 101.
Smith, S. F., D. D., Jubilee Hymn, 130.
Sonnet, Mrs. Ballard Blake, 57.
Springfield Union, quoted, 152.
Stone of Scone, The, Mrs. Hunt Candee, 71.
Stow, Mrs., S. D. Locke, Early Trustees, 63.
Sunday, before the jubilee, 9 ; after, 151.

Tyler, Prof. H. M., 148.
Tyler, Wm. S., D. D., Historical address, 107.

Williston, A. L, Esq., 6, 7, 67.

www.ingramcontent.com/pod-product-compliance
Lightning Source LLC
Chambersburg PA
CBHW022123160426
43197CB00009B/1134